Beautiful Boards

Beautiful Boards

50 Amazing Snack Boards for Any Occasion

Maegan Brown
The BakerMama

Inspiring | Educating | Creating | Entertaining

Brimming with creative inspiration, how-to projects, and useful information to enrich your everyday life, Quarto Knows is a favorite destination for those pursuing their interests and passions. Visit our site and dig deeper with our books into your area of interest: Quarto Creates, Quarto Cooks, Quarto Homes, Quarto Lives, Quarto Drives, Quarto Explores, Quarto Gifts, or Quarto Kids.

Text © 2019 by Maegan Brown

First published in 2019 by Rock Point, an imprint of The Quarto Group,
142 West 36th Street, 4th Floor, New York, NY 10018, USA
T (212) 779-4972 F (212) 779-6058 www.QuartoKnows.com

Rock Point titles are also available at discount for retail, wholesale, promotional, and bulk purchase. For details, contact the Special Sales Manager by email at specialsales@quarto.com or by mail at The Quarto Group, Attn: Special Sales Manager, 100 Cummings Center, Suite 265D, Beverly, MA 01915, USA

10 9 8 7

ISBN: 978-1-63106-647-4

Library of Congress Control Number: 2019943781

Publisher: Rage Kindelsperger
Creative Director: Laura Drew
Managing Editor: Cara Donaldson
Senior Editor: Erin Canning
Art Director: Cindy Samargia Laun
Photography: Jerrelle Guy
Cover and Interior Design: Lauren Vajda

Printed in Canada

To Brandon,

I love you. I'm so lucky to get to do life with you. Thank you for your incredible love and support always. You're my forever favorite person to share a board and bottle (or two!) of wine with.

To Baker, Bryce, Barrett, and Brookie,

You are my reason. You give me the energy and enthusiasm to live this crazy life to its fullest. Raising you is such a privilege. I hope you always feel my love and know that I'm here for you first and foremost.

To my mom and dad,

Thanks to you, I love great food and entertaining. My passion for building boards all started with the wooden lazy Susan we ate from for every meal while I was growing up. You raised me so well, and I'm so thankful for that. I love you!

To our dear friends,

Many of these boards were created with and for you. Enjoying them with you brings us the utmost joy. Our home is always open to you. Come on in and gather round, and we will toast to this beautiful life we get to support each other through.

To my dedicated followers,

Thank you for letting me inspire you. I love sharing my creations with you and connecting with you over a shared passion for feeding our loved ones well.

CONTENTS

MEET THE
BRAIN
BEHIND THE BOARDS

ABOUT MAEGAN BROWN (AKA THE BAKERMAMA)

"If you board it, they will come!" That's my motto. I strongly believe that serving food on a board truly brings people together in a special way.

I learned early on that food is an important part of our lives, from how we enjoy it to the way it nourishes us. My life has been filled with memories of wonderful meals enjoyed with family and friends. My hope is to fill our home with these same memories and raise a family who appreciates the deliciousness and the joy that food brings us.

When I was growing up, my mom would place all our meals on a wooden lazy Susan in the middle of our dining table. She still has it on her table today! We were encouraged to fill our own plates with a variety of foods and to try new things, even if we thought we wouldn't like them. Doing this made mealtimes exciting, fulfilling, and memorable. My husband, Brandon, and I have adapted the same meal concept in our home now that our kids are old enough to serve and feed themselves.

We're teaching our kids to share and make choices and have a healthy relationship with and appreciation for food. Our kids eat so much better, with little to no complaining, when they can see all their options and have the freedom to fill their own plates. Watching our kids fall in love

with fruits and vegetables and spices and get excited about combining different flavors and textures is what it's all about.

They all eat salad now because of the Build-Your-Own Cobb Salad Board (page 131) I regularly serve. My oldest, who claims he doesn't like fruit or yogurt, will happily eat both on the mornings I assemble the Build-Your-Own Parfait Board (page 109) for breakfast. And they all tend to try and like something new every time I intentionally put a new-to-them food on an Everyday Board (page 25) that we eat for snack time, dinnertime, or anytime!

Food boards have also proven to be a great way to eat and entertain for us. I think it's amazing how something as simple as how we serve our food can have such an impact on how we eat and what we eat. It's a way of serving that gives people options and awareness for what they're eating.

Our friends and family get so excited when I create a beautiful board for us to enjoy together on a casual Friday night or for a holiday celebration. When we gather around one of these boards, I notice how the experience is much different from sitting down to a more formal plated meal. People are smiling and sharing and trying everything. They're talking about the food and where it comes from and how it was made. They're truly appreciating the experience.

Assembling boards with foods people will actually eat is very important to me. I stick to my other motto of "No fluff, just the good stuff!" when it comes to building boards. The foods on the boards I create are tried and tasty. I won't put something on a board just for "looks." I don't want people to have to think whether it's there to eat or not. I love seeing everyone enjoy what's on the board as well as talking about how delicious it all is to eat.

We love opening our home and providing a place for our loved ones to gather and celebrate a special occasion or just life, and there's almost always a board involved. Whether it is an appetizer board, a dessert board, or the main meal, I truly believe that if you board it, they will come. Big or small, simple or extravagant, it's the effort spent preparing it and, more importantly, the time spent enjoying it, that matters most.

Oh, and if you invite us to your house, you better believe I'm bringing a board of some sort with me. One of my favorite gestures is to buy a reasonably priced board to build the board on that I'm bringing, and then I will leave the board, with a little note taped to the bottom of it, with the hosts as a hosting gift. It's a simple and special way to thank them for having us.

My dream for *Beautiful Boards* is to encourage you to get in the kitchen and make something memorable for your family and friends to enjoy together. Assembling a board can be overwhelming, but it shouldn't be. I'm here to inspire you to build with confidence, knowing that there are no rules when building a great board. Allow yourself to make it easy and fun so that you can relax and be present with your friends and family as everyone digs in to your amazing creation. Anything goes, and just the effort will excite everyone lucky enough to enjoy it with you.

I hope these approachable, creative, and family-friendly board ideas will change the way you think about entertaining and feeding your loved ones and that you will reach for this book again and again for any and all occasions.

All A-Board!

Maegan

THE
SNACK BOARD
MIND-SET

In my opinion, serving food on shareable boards is one of the greatest ideas in the history of eating and entertaining. It's a gesture of hospitality and appreciation for food that transcends the basic plated meal. Boards bring people together, through sharing and eating and connecting, than a traditional sit-down dinner does. And boards are just as fun to create and look at as they are to eat.

A board is usually the star of a party, whether it is for the appetizer, main course, or dessert. People automatically gravitate to and huddle around it, oohing and aahing as if it's a newborn baby, while filling up on all the goodness it has to offer. There's usually something for everyone, or at least there can be.

Boards include a variety of foods, which makes them great for a group. They allow everyone (especially kids!) to experiment with new foods as they feel empowered by being able to choose what they eat and build their own plates/meals. Even the pickiest of eaters will usually try something new and find that they actually enjoy it when grazing on a great board.

The beauty of being able to assemble a board for any occasion is that it really doesn't require much effort. You can build a beautiful board with what you have on hand in a matter of minutes. It's a mind-set of knowing what you have and what you may need. You probably already have several

ingredients that would go perfectly on your board, making great use of pantry staples and what you may have in your fridge or freezer. Boards are a great way to reinvent leftovers, clean out the fridge, and feed people without cooking.

Any snack or meal can be boarded! Whether you're planning a dinner party, football watch party, birthday party, baby shower, engagement celebration, or even just a family movie night, building a board to fit the occasion is so satisfying and sure to impress.

You can go as casual or as formal as you like when building a board, from the quick technique of piling it all on and filling in every open space to taking your time to design a festive and aesthetic masterpiece. It's all about getting creative with your food and serving it in an exciting and enticing way. We eat with our eyes first, so something as simple as forming your kids' snacks into a cute shape or overflowing a board with a stunning selection of meats and cheeses makes for a memorable eating experience that you'll want to recreate again and again.

The goal is to be able to prep the board in advance so that you can also enjoy the experience with your loved ones and have little maintenance to do throughout and minimal dishes to clean up afterward. Making a successful board does require some thought, but once you understand the concept, it will come to you as a meal and entertaining option over and over again. Just a few simple steps will give you the confidence you need to build crowd-pleasing boards:

1. **GATHER YOUR BOARD AND INGREDIENTS.** A well-stocked pantry, fridge, and freezer make building boards a breeze. Fresh fruits and veggies, prepackaged snacks, leftovers, and some store-bought items help keep it quick and simple.

2. **ASSEMBLE THE INGREDIENTS ON YOUR BOARD.** Place any serving bowls on the board first, followed by the rest of the goodies, from largest to smallest.

3. **LOAD IT UP!** A bountiful board is beautiful and inviting, so feel free to pile it up and fill in all the nooks and crannies with goodies that are sure to be enjoyed.

4. **OPEN YOUR HOME TO FRIENDS AND FAMILY.** You want to share your beautiful and delicious board creations, of course.

5. **RELAX.** You did all the work in advance, so you can be present with your loved ones while they enjoy your amazing creation instead of in the kitchen prepping more food.

6. **ENJOY THE DELICIOUSNESS AND THE TIME WITH YOUR LOVED ONES.**

No matter what your kitchen skill level is, you can do this! The only rule is that there are NO RULES! From building it to serving it, just get creative, have fun, and most importantly, enjoy!

TIPS FOR A CLASSIC CHARCUTERIE AND CHEESE BOARD (ALSO SEE PAGE 41)

- I recommend 3 or 4 types of meat for a smaller crowd and 4 or 5 types for a larger crowd. If the board is an appetizer, estimate 2 to 3 ounces (56 to 84 g) of meat per person. If the board is the main meal, estimate 3 to 5 ounces (85 to 142 g) of meat per person. All meats should be thinly sliced for charcuterie serving. Meats should be taken out just 15 to 20 minutes before serving.

- I recommend 3 or 4 types of cheese for a smaller crowd and 4 or 5 types for a larger crowd. If the board is an appetizer, estimate 1 ounce (28 g) of each cheese per person. If the board is the main meal, estimate 1½ ounces (42 g) of each cheese per person. To get the full flavor and texture of the cheeses, I recommend taking them out of the fridge 30 minutes to an hour before serving. Keep them wrapped until you're ready to place them on the board so they don't dry out. You can slice or chunk some of the cheeses on the board ahead of time for easier access when you have a large crowd. A cheese board can sit out for a couple hours once your guests arrive.

- There are many flavors and textures you can include on a good charcuterie and cheese board. For the meats, choose from a selection of smoked, dry-cured, firm, and soft. When selecting cheeses, have a variety of firm, semisoft, creamy, crumbly, smoked, and/or stinky. For the accompaniments, try to include crunchy (crackers), salty (crackers and nuts), sweet (honey, jam, fruit, nuts), and tangy (mustard, olives, and anything pickled).

- You know your crowd, so if they're big eaters, round up. If they're not, or if you're serving lots of other things, round down.

- Always add fruit such as apple and pear slices to the board last. You can cover them with a damp paper towel or brush with lemon juice to delay browning.

- I like to offer a red and white wine along with the board.

WHAT YOU'LL NEED

(BOARDS AND MORE)

I know you're excited to get to all the beautiful and delicious boards in this book, but let's first talk about the tools of the trade. There are so many types and shapes of boards and other serving utensils that you could get lost or, even worse, bored. But have no fear for I have a simple rule for you: just use it!

BOARDS

Although I suggest a certain type or shape of board with the board ideas in this book, you can use whatever you own and it will turn out great. However, if you are starting from scratch and need some boards for your arsenal, here are a few suggestions.

There are a lot of different board materials you can choose from, including marble, stone, and slate, but my favorite is a traditional wooden board. I like boards that are made of hardwoods, such as acacia, maple, oak, and cherry. Acacia is a great option if you don't want to spend a fortune on a board.

If you are going to have only one board, I would go with a large 20-inch (51cm) round wooden board. I love the look of a round board and you want something large enough to be able to entertain at least eight people. Next, I suggest getting a large rectangular board, one that is approximately 20 × 12 or 14 inches (51 × 30 or 35cm). The third board to add to your collection would be a smaller rectangular or round board for serving two to four people. After you have those three boards, you can begin to build your collection with unique shapes, sizes, and materials. But most of all, have fun and don't worry if you don't have the perfect board, because it is all about the food and company anyway!

BOARD MAINTENANCE

I could tell you to use expensive board cleaners and polishers to keep your boards looking like new, but the reality is, don't stress over how perfect your boards look because at the end of the night, they will be covered in cheese crumbles, smears of spreads, loose vegetables, and maybe even a splash of wine. After the meal or evening is over, I simply scrub mine with hot water and dish soap, and then immediately dry it. If there is a stain, I give it a little elbow grease, and that generally works. There are a variety of store-bought and homemade stain remover solutions you can try if the stain is being difficult. Finally, I do treat my boards with food-safe mineral oil and wax them every three to six months or when they start to look a bit rough or dry.

BEYOND THE BOARD

In addition to the board(s), you will need a variety of serving bowls or ramekins for dips and spreads. I own a variety of small porcelain and glass bowls and ramekins in different shapes and sizes. My favorite sizes are 3 ounces (84 g) for dips and olives and 1 ounce (28 g) for spreads, honeys, and jams.

You will also need to have a selection of knives, spreaders, and spoons for serving. A spade knife is great for cutting chunks or wedges of hard cheeses. A soft cheese knife is perfect for spreading soft cheeses, like Brie, on crackers. A flat cheese knife is used to cut crumbly cheeses or to cut and chip firm cheeses. Cheese planes are nice for cutting during preparation or to serve on the board. I like to have a cheese knife for each cheese, a spreader for each jam or spread, and a honey dipper for drizzling honey.

EVERYTHING YOU NEED TO GET STARTED BUILDING BOARDS

1 round wooden board (20 inches, or 51cm)

2 medium serving bowls (8 to 10 ounces, or 227 to 283 g, each)

2 small ramekins or serving bowls (3 ounces, or 84 g, each)

2 mini ramekins or serving bowls (1 ounce, or 28 g, each)

4 small Mason jars (4 ounces, or 113 g, each)

1 spade knife

1 soft cheese knife

1 flat cheese knife

1 cheese plane

4 cheese spreaders

2 extra-small spoons

1 honey dipper

Serving utensils, if necessary

OFF-THE-BOARD SUPPLIES

Small serving plates

Napkins (cloth or fun, festive paper ones to fit the occasion)

Toothpicks

Forks, spoons, and/or knives, if necessary

Small slate cheese markers/labels

BUILDING
AND
SERVING
THE BOARDS

Here's what you need to know about assembling a board, including tips on what to keep stocked, how much to have of each item, and how best to serve it, store it, and transport it, if necessary.

STOCKING

A well-stocked pantry and fridge makes building boards such an easy and convenient option come meal or snack time. I like to buy our favorite snacks in bulk so that we always have them on hand when a board is in order. Here's a list of what I try to always keep stocked:

- **FRUITS:** apples, grapes, strawberries

- **VEGGIES:** baby carrots, snap peas, broccoli, olives, pickles

- **CHEESES:** cheddar cheese cracker cuts, good-quality white cheddar, creamy Brie, goat cheese, string cheese

- **MEATS:** good-quality pepperoni, sliced turkey, a nice salami stick for slicing into thin rounds

- **DIPS AND SPREADS:** honey, hummus, ranch dressing, peanut butter, fruit jam, salsa

- **SAVORY SNACKS:** crackers, pretzels, chips, nuts, popcorn

- **SWEET SNACKS:** dried fruit, yogurt-covered pretzels, chocolate-covered almonds, mini cookies

When planning out your board, choose foods that keep well at room temperature. Most boards are intended to be quick to make yet slow to enjoy. This is about grazing and snacking, so make sure the foods can last the length of your meal or get-together.

QUANTITIES

A common question is how much of each item will you need for the board so that you have enough, but not too much. This all depends on how many people you're serving, the course you're serving the board for, and how hungry your crowd is when you serve it.

The more choices you offer on the board, the smaller the individual portion should be for each item, because most people will want to try at least one or some of everything on the board. So, when you're offering several choices on the board, make sure they are bite-size. Anticipate which foods will be more popular and plan to add more of them.

For a snack board as a starter, I'd recommend an average per person of 2 ounces (56 g) of cheese, 2 ounces (56 g) of meat, 4 or 5 crackers, 3 bites of fruit, 3 bites of vegetables, 1 tablespoon (9 g) of nuts, and 1 tablespoon (20 g) of honey or jam per person. On a snack board as a main course, I'd recommend an average of 4 ounces (112 g) of cheese,

4 ounces (112 g) of meat, 8 to 10 crackers, 6 bites of fruit, 6 bites of vegetables, 2 tablespoons (18 g) of nuts, and 2 tablespoons (40 g) of honey or jam.

For meal boards, such as the Pancake Board (page 107) and Barbecue Board (page 135), plan the quantities based on the number of people you're serving. If you were to build a plate with the items on the board, determine how much of each food you would put on your plate, and then multiply that by the number of people you're serving, keeping in mind that everyone's appetites and preferences are different. Also, make sure you calculate children's portions separate from adult portions.

Again, it all depends on the occasion, timing, and how hungry your crowd is. You know your people best, but keep in mind that it's better to have extra than not enough. You can always store the leftovers for another board the next day.

BUILDING

With almost every board, I recommend placing any serving bowls on the board first in various locations so the board feels balanced. Then place the rest of the ingredients, from largest to smallest. If there are items on the board that need to be served warm, plan to put them on last. Also, plan to put any sliced apples or pears on the board last because they tend to brown quickly. You can cover sliced apples and pears with a damp paper towel until ready to serve, or brush them with lemon juice.

Place the ingredients that complement each other or that pair well together next to each other on the board. Simple touches like fanning the crackers around the serving bowls, drizzling the hummus with olive oil, and adding fresh herbs that enhance the foods make the board all the more beautiful and inviting.

Try to keep moisture-rich ingredients like fresh-cut fruit and pickled vegetables (drained and patted dry) apart from crispy foods like crackers and nuts, so they don't get soggy.

SERVING

In terms of serving a board, you can let your guests gather around it and reach in free-for-all style, encouraging them to mingle and come back for more at their leisure. Or you can seat everyone with the board in the middle of the table and conduct a more proper meal that's all about sharing and filling their plates with whatever they'd like from the board.

If entertaining and making an appetizer board, it's best to have the board out when your guests arrive so you can immediately greet them and start mingling without having to be in the kitchen still building it. If you're building the board for a family dinner or a last-minute hangout with your closest friends, build it with them. They'll probably enjoy helping you and getting creative with what and where to put things on the board. Several of the boards in this book can be made completely or partially in advance, so there's no stress when you're ready to serve it. See tips for storing and transporting the boards if you're planning to make it in advance.

Perishable foods should not stand at room temperature for longer than about two hours, so plan ahead if your gathering is expected to last longer. You can have refills ready to go in the fridge so you, or even your best guest, can easily refill a food item that's running low.

Use the board to spark conversations throughout the gathering. People generally love talking about food: where it's from, where you bought it, what they like or don't like about something, their favorite foods, and foods they've never tried before; the best is when you learn about a food you've yet to try.

STORING

If you'd like to prep your board in advance, place everything on it that can withstand refrigeration and then cover just the top of the board with plastic wrap before placing it in the refrigerator. You'll have to wait to add the crunchy snacks, such as crackers and nuts, so they don't get soggy, along with anything that needs to be heated, such as pancakes or pizza rolls, until just before serving the board. If you do refrigerate a fully or partially made board, be sure to set it out about 30 minutes before serving, so the food, especially any cheese, starts coming to room temperature for best flavor.

TIMING

The amount of time it takes to build each board depends on the prep of the ingredients and the complexity of the design. Your everyday snack board is intended to take about 15 minutes, using items you readily have on hand. The holiday shapes will take longer based on your precision and speed. What's most important is that you don't take the board or yourself too seriously. I encourage you to have fun and enjoy the process as much as the moment you present it to your loved ones.

TRANSPORTING

I've found the best way to prepare a board for transportation is to lay one or two large pieces of heavy-duty foil on the counter—the foil should be big enough to wrap up and over the completed board. Place the board on the foil, and then start building it. Once the board is built, cover any serving bowls with plastic wrap so things don't fall into or spill out of the bowl. Bring the foil up over the board, so it's completely covering all the ingredients, and fold together to create a tented cover. Press in on the foil around the edges of the board to hold the ingredients in place and prevent major shifting.

ANYTIME
BOARDS

You can make any occasion go from good to great with a beautiful and delicious food board. All of these anytime boards have a wonderful variety of goodies to make everyone happy. They are easy and quick to build, making them perfect for any gathering, big or small. My family knows that if I don't have the time or the ingredients to cook a meal, there's going to be a great board built with what we have on hand. So, go ahead and invite the neighbors over for a dinner of snacks on Sunday night, or put the kids to bed early so you can enjoy some peace and quiet with your partner—a beautiful board can be built at a moment's notice.

EVERYDAY
BOARD

SERVES 6-8 PEOPLE ⎰ USE A 20 × 13-INCH (51 × 33 CM) BOARD

Use whatever you have on hand in the fridge or pantry to create a fast, simple, and healthy snack board for lunchtime, dinnertime, or anytime! A snack board is a great way to reinvent leftovers or introduce foods that diners might not otherwise try. It's the best way to feed people without having to cook. Everyone gets excited when a bountiful and colorful snack board is served. From salty to sweet and crunchy to chewy, it's pretty much a party for the palate. A snack board like this one should take you 15 to 20 minutes to build with foods you already have on hand in your pantry or fridge, making it perfect for every day.

¾ cup (180 g) hummus (store-bought or see recipe on page 156)

¾ cup (180 ml) ranch dressing

¾ cup (180 ml) salsa (store-bought or see recipe on page 157)

10 to 12 orange cheddar cheese cracker cuts

10 to 12 white cheddar cheese cracker cuts

1 cup (120 g) Colby Jack cheese cubes

6 slices turkey meat, rolled

12 slices pepperoni

1 small bunch green grapes

1 small bunch red grapes

8 to 10 multigrain chips

12 pretzel chips

12 buttery round crackers

8 to 10 yogurt-covered pretzels

½ apple, thinly sliced

10 baby carrots

12 to 14 snow peas

6 to 8 cherry tomatoes, cut in half

8 dried apricots

16 to 18 raspberries

8 to 10 pickle chips

8 pitted green olives

½ cup (75 g) trail mix with M&M'S

1 cup (16 g) popcorn

1. Start by putting the hummus, ranch dressing, and salsa in small bowls and place the bowls across the board.

2. Arrange the orange cheddar cheese cracker cuts toward the top of the board, the white cheddar cracker cuts at the bottom of the board, and the Colby Jack cheese cubes in the middle. Place the turkey slice rolls and the pepperoni on the board.

3. Arrange the green and red grapes, followed by the multigrain chips, pretzel chips, round crackers, and yogurt-covered pretzels in various locations across the board, fanning them around the serving bowls wherever possible.

4. Arrange the apple slices, baby carrots, snow peas, cherry tomatoes, dried apricots, raspberries, pickle slices, and green olives on the board in open spaces.

5. Finish the board by adding the trail mix and popcorn.

AFTER SCHOOL
BOARD

SERVES 6-8 PEOPLE { USE A 15-INCH (38 CM) ROUND BOARD

Whether you're just feeding your kids after a long day at school or a houseful of preschool friends playing the afternoon away, you can make snack time fun and yummy with this interactive board that lets the little ones build their own "ants on a log" or "fish in a river," all while practicing their spelling with alphabet-shaped cookies on the side. It's a simple way to bring everybody together and talk about the day.

½ cup (120 g) hummus

½ cup (130 g) peanut butter

5 celery ribs, cut in thirds

12 white cheese shapes (precut or cut with a small cookie cutter)

12 orange cheese shapes (precut or cut with a small cookie cutter)

1 cup (120 g) Colby Jack cheese cubes

20 Oatmeal Chocolate Chip Bites (see recipe on page 149)

12 red grapes, cut in half

12 green grapes, cut in half

2 mandarin oranges, peeled and segments separated

1 cup (75 g) snap peas

1 cup (120 g) baby carrots

½ cup (60 g) dried cranberries

1 cup (60 g) fish-shaped crackers

1 cup (140 g) snack mix (store-bought or see recipe on page 149)

1 cup (100 g) veggie straws or sticks

1 cup (16 g) white cheddar corn puffs

1 cup (120 g) yogurt-covered pretzels

½ red apple, sliced

2 cups (240 g) alphabet-shaped cookies, on the side to spell with and eat

1. Put the hummus and peanut butter in small serving bowls and place the bowls on the board.

2. Arrange half the celery around the hummus bowl and half around the peanut butter bowl.

3. Place the cheese shapes on either side of the board and the cheese cubes in the center of the board between the bowls of hummus and peanut butter.

4. Add 10 of the oatmeal chocolate chip bites to the board. (Save the remaining 10 to refill the board if needed.)

5. Place the halved grapes, orange segments, snap peas, and carrots on the board.

6. Add the dried cranberries near the bowl of peanut butter and the fish-shaped crackers near the bowl of hummus, encouraging the kids to create "ants on a log" with the celery, peanut butter, and dried cranberries and "fish in a river" with the celery, hummus, and fish-shaped crackers as they snack.

7. Pile the snack mix near the center of the board.

8. Place the veggie straws, corn puffs, yogurt-covered pretzels, and apple slices in the gaps across the board.

9. Put the alphabet-shaped cookies in a bowl to the side and encourage the kids to spell with them.

CHIPS AND DIPS
BOARD

SERVES 10+ PEOPLE ⟩ USE A 26 × 13-INCH (66 × 38 CM) BOARD

I dip, you dip, we all dip our way across this epic appetizer board with an amazing assortment of dips and chips to keep everyone coming back for more. This is one of the easiest boards to build for a crowd. It's great before taco night, during the big game, or for a wedding shower fiesta. Get your dip on!

2½ cups (600 g) guacamole (store-bought or see recipe on page 157)

1 cup (240 g) pico de gallo (store-bought or see recipe on page 158)

1 cup (240 g) queso (store-bought or see recipe on page 158)

1 cup (240 g) roasted tomatillo salsa verde

1 cup (240 g) sour cream spinach dip (store-bought or see recipe on page 159)

¾ cup (180 g) bean dip

¾ cup (180 g) French onion dip

¾ cup (180 g) hummus (store-bought or see recipe on page 156)

6 cups (360 g) multicolored tortilla chips, divided by color if desired

2 cups (120 g) blue corn tortilla chips

2 cups (120 g) blue corn scoop chips

2 cups (120 g) flax multigrain chips

2 cups (120 g) kettle-cooked potato chips

2 cups (120 g) wavy potato chips

2 cups (120 g) Fritos corn chips

1. Put all the dips in small serving bowls and place the bowls across the board.

2. Fill in the rest of the space on the board with the chips.

FRUIT AND DIPS
BOARD

SERVES 12+ PEOPLE ⟩ USE A 20-INCH (51 CM) ROUND BOARD

This breathtaking board of beautiful fresh fruits with a variety of dips to accompany them makes for a stunning addition to any brunch, shower, or summer soirée. It's so gorgeous to look at and even better to graze on. This board proves that offering healthy options when entertaining doesn't have to be boring.

1 whole pineapple

1 cup (125 g) raspberries, divided

1½ cups (225 g) blueberries, divided

1½ cups (225 g) blackberries, divided

1½ cups (360 g) chocolate pudding

¾ cup (180 ml) caramel dip

1½ cups (360 g) plain or vanilla
  Greek yogurt

¾ cup (180 g) mixed berry
  whipped cream cheese

1 cup (150 g) chunky granola

2 cups (300 g) red grapes,
  in bunches

2 cups (300 g) green grapes,
  in bunches

2 medium oranges, sliced into wedges

12 small watermelon wedges,
  with rinds

1 mango, peeled, pitted,
  and thinly sliced

2 kiwi, peeled and thinly sliced

1 medium starfruit, sliced

15 whole strawberries

1 red apple, thinly sliced

1 cup (150 g) fresh whole cherries,
  with stems

2 bananas, peeled and sliced

1. Vertically slice the pineapple in half, keeping the stem on one half. Hollow out the half with the stem to be used as a bowl. Reserve the pineapple flesh. Place the pineapple bowl in the center of the board.

2. Cut the reserved pineapple flesh into chunks. Mix the pineapple chunks with ¼ cup (38 g) of the raspberries, ¼ cup (31 g) of the blueberries, and ¼ cup (38 g) of the blackberries. Put the pineapple and berry fruit mixture into the hollowed-out pineapple bowl.

3. Put the chocolate pudding, caramel dip, yogurt, cream cheese, and granola in small serving bowls and place the bowls across the board.

4. Arrange the grape bunches on the board, followed by the orange slices, watermelon wedges, and sliced mango.

5. Fan the kiwi slices around the yogurt bowl, the starfruit around the cream cheese bowl, the strawberries around the chocolate pudding bowl, and the apple slices around the caramel dip bowl.

6. Place the cherries near the top of the pineapple stem and the banana slices next to the cherries.

7. Fill in the gaps on the board with the remaining ¾ cup (94 g) raspberries, 1¼ cups (190 g) blueberries, and 1¼ cups (190 g) blackberries.

GLUTEN-FREE
BOARD

You'd never guess this snack board was completely gluten-free just by looking at it. There are tons of gluten-free snack options available these days, which makes it easy to assemble a great spread for everyone to enjoy, whether they follow a gluten-free diet or not. With plenty of naturally gluten-free snacks, such as cheeses, fruits, veggies, and nuts, and several tasty packaged food options, such as pretzels, crackers, chips, and popcorn, this board is a snacking sensation!

¾ cup (180 g) salsa (store-bought or see recipe on page 157)

¾ cup (180 g) spinach and kale Greek yogurt dip (store-bought or see recipe on page 159)

10 to 12 mixed olives

¼ cup (65 g) creamy peanut butter or almond butter

¼ cup (80 g) honey

24 gluten-free pretzel sticks

1 small bunch green grapes

1 wedge (4 ounces, or 112 g) blue cheese

½ cup (60 g) Swiss cheese cubes

6 rolls mozzarella wrapped with prosciutto

6 rolls mozzarella wrapped with salami

15 multiseed gluten-free crackers

15 rice crackers

20 gluten-free tortilla chips

1½ cups (90 g) vegetable chips

18 to 20 roasted plantain chips

5 small radishes, sliced

6 petite carrots, peeled

½ bell pepper (any color), cut into strips

¼ red apple, thinly sliced

¼ green apple, thinly sliced

¾ cup (12 g) popped popcorn

½ cup (75 g) whole roasted almonds

1. Put the salsa, Greek yogurt dip, and olives in small serving bowls and place the bowls across the board. Put the peanut butter, honey, and pretzel sticks into small jars and place the jars on the board.

2. Arrange the grapes in the bottom-left corner of the board.

3. Place the blue cheese wedge and Swiss cheese cubes on the board, followed by the meat and cheese rolls.

4. Fan the multiseed crackers around the Greek yogurt dip bowl and the rice crackers around the blue cheese and olives.

5. Place the tortilla chips around the salsa, then arrange the vegetable chips on the top of the board and the plantain chips on the bottom of the board.

6. Fan the radish slices around the other side of the Greek yogurt dip bowl. Add the carrots, bell pepper slices, and red and green apple slices to the board.

7. Fill in the gaps on the board with the popcorn and almonds.

VEGAN
BOARD

SERVES 6-8 PEOPLE ⟩ USE A 12-INCH (30 CM) RUSTIC ROUND BOARD

Wow vegans and non-vegans alike with this beautiful board of plant-based snacks. Fig "salami," cashew "cheese" dip, and delicious cheddar-style "cheese" slices are just a few of the tasty alternatives among the abundance of veggies that make this vegan board beautiful to the eyes and palate.

⅓ cup (80 g) beet hummus (store-bought or see recipe on page 156)

⅓ cup (80 g) store-bought dairy-free cucumber and basil dip

⅓ cup (80 g) cashew cheese dip alternative

1 pistachio fig salami log (6.4 ounces, or 180 g), sliced

3 or 4 slices dairy-free cheddar-style cheese slices, cut into quarters

½ medium cucumber, thinly sliced

3 large gluten-free Norwegian-style cracker crisps, broken into smaller pieces

15 rice crackers

8 petite multicolored carrots, peeled and sliced in half lengthwise

16 asparagus tips

1 bunch broccolini, end trimmed

8 small purple endive leaves

8 small yellow endive leaves

5 radishes, cut in quarters

10 mini heirloom tomatoes, cut in half

⅓ cup (35 g) mixed olives

½ cup (75 g) candied walnuts

½ cup (75 g) sesame honey cashews

1. Put the beet hummus, cucumber and basil dip, and cashew cheese dip in small serving bowls and place the bowls across the board.

2. Fan the fig salami and cheddar-style cheese slices on opposite sides of the bottom of the board.

3. Fan the sliced cucumber around the cucumber and basil dip bowl.

4. Add the broken cracker crisps and rice crackers to the board.

5. Arrange the carrots, asparagus tips, and broccolini on the board, then tuck the purple and yellow endive leaves onto opposite sides of the center of the board.

6. Fill in the gaps on the board with the radishes, halved tomatoes, olives, walnuts, and cashews.

DATE NIGHT IN
BOARD

SERVES 2 PEOPLE ⟩ USE A 16 × 6-INCH (40.6 × 15 CM) BOARD WITH A HANDLE

Keep date night simple yet special by staying in and enjoying each other's company, along with a board built with the best meats, cheeses, and accompaniments. This is our favorite way to spend a Friday and/or Saturday night. We put the kids to bed and then build the board together. We've done this for so long that we've perfected our preferences when it comes to which cheeses and meats we enjoy most together along with the nibbles that accompany them. We sit for hours enjoying each other, this board, and our favorite bottle of wine. An evening well spent!

2 tablespoons (30 g) cherry preserves

2 tablespoons (40 g) honey

2 tablespoons (30 g) fig jam

2 tablespoons (22 g) whole-grain mustard

4 thin slices soppressata

4 thin slices prosciutto (I recommend Casella's prosciutto speciale)

4 thin slices salami (I recommend Olli Salumeria's Toscano salami)

4 thin slices coppa

3 ounces (84 g) aged white cheddar

3 ounces (84 g) aged Gouda

3 ounces (84 g) Manchego

3 ounces (84 g) triple crème cheese

¼ cup (35 g) Marcona almonds

4 dried apricots

¼ cup (30 g) mixed olives

¼ cup (30 g) red grapes

4 thin slices apple (Red Delicious or Honeycrisp)

1 fresh fig, cut in half

1. Put the cherry preserves, honey, fig jam, and mustard into small serving bowls.

2. Place the following meat, cheese, and spread combinations beside each other along the board so they can be enjoyed together:

   - The soppressata, white cheddar, and cherry preserves pair best together.
   - The prosciutto, aged Gouda, and honey pair best together.
   - The salami, Manchego, and fig jam pair best together.
   - The coppa, triple crème, and whole-grain mustard pair best together.

3. Add the Marcona almonds, dried apricots, mixed olives, red grapes, apple slices, and fig as accompaniments across the board.

ENTERTAINING
AND
SPECIAL
OCCASION
BOARDS

I strongly believe that any gathering of friends and family is a special occasion, a reason to celebrate. And special occasions call for special spreads. These are the boards that are sure to wow your crowd with their beauty and deliciousness. They're inviting and celebratory. Whether it's a birthday, the big game, an engagement, or just a special Saturday night dinner with great friends, these stunning boards will keep everyone happily grazing for hours.

CHARCUTERIE
AND
CHEESE
BOARD

SERVES 6-8 PEOPLE ⟩ USE A 30 × 15-INCH (76 × 38 CM) BOARD

Nothing elevates a gathering more than a beautifully presented charcuterie and cheese board. It's pretty much a given that if you walk into our house for a dinner party, you will be greeted by a big board covered in a delicious assortment of meats, cheeses, and nibbles that are a feast for the eyes as well as the palate. It's our favorite way to entertain and is a guaranteed way to impress our guests without a lot of stress. It allows us the opportunity to greet our guests and get the party started right away. This board can be made as an appetizer or the main event. Quantities truly depend on what course the board is being served for and how many you're serving. One thing I always make sure to do is encourage our guests to dig right in so they're not intimidated by it. I love how guests can create all sorts of combinations to keep the experience unique and entertaining. The only rule is to enjoy!

2 tablespoons (30 g) fig jam

2 tablespoons (30 g) strawberry preserves

2 tablespoons (30 g) apricot preserves

2 tablespoons (22 g) whole-grain seeded mustard

2-inch (5 cm) portion of honeycomb with honey

⅓ cup (35 g) mixed olives

8 ounces (227 g) aged white cheddar

8 ounces (227 g) Manchego

8 ounces (227 g) aged Gouda

5 ounces (140 g) triple crème cheese

5 ounces (140 g) blue Stilton cheese

12 slices coppa

10 slices prosciutto

10 slices piccante salami

10 slices Bavarian salami

4 slices mortadella

1 large bunch red grapes

1 large bunch green grapes

10 whole-grain crackers

15 seeded crackers

15 fruit and nut crackers or crisps

10 salted crackers

¼ cup (38 g) Marcona almonds

¼ cup (38 g) candied pecans

¼ cup (38 g) sesame honey cashews

½ cup (65 g) dried apricots

¼ cup (30 g) dried cherries

5 dried orange slices

⅓ cup (60 g) cornichons

½ pear, thinly sliced

½ yellow apple, thinly sliced

½ red apple, thinly sliced

3 fresh figs, cut in half

(CONTINUED)

1. Put the fig jam, strawberry preserves, apricot preserves, mustard, honeycomb with honey, and mixed olives into small serving bowls and place the bowls across the board. Arrange the cheeses on the board.

2. Arrange the meats on the board, followed by the red and green grape bunches.

3. Fan the crackers around a few of the serving bowls, around a cheese wedge, and in little stacks across the board.

4. Fill in the gaps with the nuts, dried fruits, cornichons, pear slices, apple slices, and figs. It's perfectly fine for items to touch each other and overlap.

RAINBOW
BOARD

Taste the rainbow with this colorful selection of fresh fruits and veggies in a beautiful rainbow shape, complete with cloud crackers and a pot of gold chocolates. Serve this cute board with a fruit dip, ranch dressing, and/or hummus on the side for a deliciously healthy addition to any celebration. It's sure to brighten everyone's day!

16 round water crackers

2 cups (340 g) halved strawberries

1 cup (116 g) thinly sliced radish

1 large red bell pepper, cut into strips

1 cup (150 g) raspberries

1 cup (150 g) halved cherry tomatoes

1 navel orange, cut into slices with the peel on

5 mini orange bell peppers, thinly sliced

10 orange baby carrots

10 orange cherry tomatoes

10 yellow baby carrots, halved

10 yellow cherry tomatoes

1 medium mango, peeled, pitted, and cut into chunks

12 small broccolini or broccoli tips

10 asparagus tips

10 green grapes

10 kiwi berries, cut in half

10 mini cucumber slices

12 blackberries

½ cup (75 g) blueberries

8 black grapes, cut in half

5 cherries, pitted and cut in half

5 red grapes, cut in half

4 petite purple carrots, cut in half lengthwise

30 Rolo candies

Fruit dip, ranch dressing, and/or hummus (store-bought or see recipe on page 156), on the side, for dipping (optional)

1. Place the water crackers on the board to create the clouds at the end of the rainbow's arc, 8 on each side.

2. To create each colored arc, you will mix together each colored food across the arc. Make the red arc with the strawberries, radishes, red bell pepper, raspberries, and cherry tomatoes.

(CONTINUED)

3. Make the orange arc with the orange slices, orange bell pepper, orange baby carrots, and orange cherry tomatoes.

4. Make the yellow arc with the yellow baby carrots, yellow cherry tomatoes, and mango chunks.

5. Make the green arc with the broccolini, asparagus tips, green grapes, kiwi berries, and cucumber slices.

6. Make the blue arc with the blackberries, blueberries, and black grapes.

7. Make the purple arc with the cherries, red grapes, and purple carrots.

8. Put the Rolo candies in a black bowl and place the bowl under the crackers on the right side of the rainbow.

9. Serve the bowls of fruit dip, ranch dressing, and/or hummus on the side for dipping fruits and veggies, if desired.

BIRTHDAY DESSERT
BOARD

SERVES 10+ PEOPLE | USE A 20-INCH (51 CM) ROUND BOARD

Birthday wishes do come true with this festive board covered in every sweet, sprinkled treat you could dream of! It's a masterpiece made up of simple homemade and store-bought goodies. The great thing about this birthday dessert board is that you can customize it with the birthday person's favorite sweet treats and colors, or just stick to this bright, colorful sprinkled design that's sure to delight everyone at the party, especially the person being celebrated!

1 bag (12 ounces, or 336 g) pink candy melts

12 honey wheat pretzel twists

2 tablespoons (20 g) pastel confetti sprinkles

1 package (16 ounces, or 454 g) vanilla candy coating (such as CandiQuik brand), divided

10 donut holes

4 tablespoons (40 g) rainbow sprinkles, divided

6 large strawberries

1 decorated party cake (6 inches, or 15 cm, round), store-bought or homemade (I used a double-layer vanilla cake with white frosting and sprinkles from the bakery section at my local grocery store)

4 cups (120 g) Birthday Snack Mix (see recipe on page 150)

5 small store-bought confetti cookie sandwiches

2 cups (32 g) birthday cake popcorn or sweet glazed popcorn with confetti sprinkles

6 store-bought mini cupcakes with confetti sprinkles

10 vanilla cake balls

5 pink-frosted and sprinkled soft sugar cookies

12 squares birthday cake white chocolate candy bar or any festive white chocolate candy bar

12 chocolate-vanilla sandwich cookies

8 Birthday Cake Rice Krispies Treats

14 festively decorated yogurt-covered pretzels

Birthday cake topper and candles, for the party cake (optional)

1. Melt the pink candy melts according to the package directions. Make sure not to over-melt the candy coating because it will burn and become too thick to stir and coat the mix evenly.

2. Dip the honey wheat pretzel twists halfway in pink candy coating and sprinkle with pastel confetti sprinkles. Let set completely.

3. Melt the vanilla candy coating according to the package directions. Make sure not to over-melt the candy coating because it will burn and become too thick to stir and coat the mix evenly.

4. Dip the donut holes halfway in the vanilla candy coating and sprinkle with 2 tablespoons (20 g) of the rainbow sprinkles. Let set completely.

5. Dip the strawberries halfway in the vanilla candy coating and sprinkle with the remaining 2 tablespoons (20 g) rainbow sprinkles. Let set completely.

6. Place the party cake in the middle of the board.

7. Fan out the epic selection of sprinkled and colorful treats from the cake however you like, making sure to fill in any gaps.

8. Top the cake with the birthday cake topper and candles, if desired!

UNICORN
BOARD

Do you believe in magic? If not, you certainly will after creating and enjoying this magical unicorn board filled with the sweetest of treats that will make all your snacking dreams come true. Unicorns and rainbows are all the rage, so what's not to love about an adorable unicorn face adorned with a horn, ears, eyelashes, and even some blushing cheeks.

1 sugar ice-cream cone

1 container (12 ounces, or 336 g) whipped fluffy white frosting, divided

1 container (2 ounces, or 56 g) gold sugar sprinkles

12 Birthday Cake Rice Krispies Treats, cut in half, divided

2 cups (60 g) candy-coated popcorn

½ bag (6 ounces, or 168 g) pink candy melts

1 black licorice lace, for the facial features

10 tiny pink star-shaped sprinkles, for the blushing cheeks

10 to 12 pastel twisted marshmallow strands, for the mane

22 to 24 multicolored marshmallows

15 mini rainbow Twizzlers Twizted Strawberry Blast Pull 'n' Peel candy

18 candy-coated and rainbow-sprinkled pretzels

¼ cup (120 g) Jelly Belly Smoothie Blend jelly beans

12 rainbow lollipops

16 pink wafer cookies

15 white-striped cookies

¼ cup (120 g) Tropical Skittles

1. Coat the sugar cone with some of the whipped white frosting and immediately sprinkle it with the gold sugar sprinkles. Let dry until set on a plate. This will become the unicorn's horn.

2. Cut 2 of the Rice Krispies Treats into triangles and spread one side of each with the whipped white frosting. Let dry until set. These will become the unicorn's ears.

3. Lay the popcorn flat on a piece of parchment paper.

4. Melt the pink candy melts according to the package directions. Transfer the melted candy coating to a quart-size plastic bag and cut a tiny piece off one of the bottom corners of the bag. Drizzle the candy coating over the popcorn. Let dry until set.

5. Evenly spread the remaining frosting onto an 8-inch (20 cm) round white plate with a small rim for the unicorn's face.

6. Cut the strand of black licorice lace to create the eyelashes and smile on the face. Place the pink star sprinkles on the frosting as the blushing cheeks.

7. Lay the marshmallow strands around the top and sides of the face/plate to create the unicorn's mane.

8. Arrange the multicolored marshmallows from the face/plate down toward the bottom-left corner of the board.

9. Set the remaining 10 Rice Krispies Treats to the right of the marshmallows and work your way around the unicorn's face with the snacks in this order: Pull 'n' Peel Twizzlers, coated pretzels, jelly beans, lollipops, pink wafer cookies, popcorn, white-striped cookies, and Skittles.

10. Place the sugar cone horn in the center of the unicorn's head. Use the coated Rice Krispies Treats triangles to create the unicorn's ears on top of the hair.

PRINCESS
BOARD

SERVES 12+ PEOPLE ⟩ USE A 20 × 13-INCH (51 × 33 CM) BOARD WITH A LIP

Once upon a time, your little one wished they were a princess and you can't deny them this fairy tale. Whether it's their birthday or an afternoon playdate with special guests, you can make their royal dreams come true with this dazzling princess board. All the pink treats one could wish for, along with fruit wands, play crowns, and even a gummy frog coming in for the kiss, will make their magical moment sweet and special.

12 wooden or metal skewers (7 inches, or 18 cm, each)

12 cute paper straws (at least 7½ inches, or 19 cm, each)

24 strawberries, stems removed

24 red grapes

12 star-shaped watermelon cutouts (I used a cookie cutter)

1¼ cups (20 g) birthday cake popcorn

18 large strawberry marshmallows

1 bag (12 ounces, or 336 g) pink candy melts

½ cup (75 g) pink sugar sprinkles, divided

1 bag (12 ounces, or 336 g) white candy melts, divided

1 cup (25 g) Bugles

12 pink wafer cookies

½ cup (75 g) pink pearl sprinkles

1 cup (165 g) pink M&M'S

1 cup (165 g) pink jelly beans

24 pink flower-shaped cookies

24 pink strawberry yogurt–coated pretzels

36 Strawberry Pocky biscuit sticks

¼ cup (40 g) pink, purple, and white yogurt–covered raisins

30 square-shaped fruit jellies

½ cup (30 g) pink fish-shaped crackers

Play princess crowns, for decorating (optional)

Large frog gummy, for decorating (optional)

1. To make the fruit wands, stick a skewer through a cute paper straw. Poke the skewer through a strawberry, then a grape, another strawberry, and another grape before sticking the star-shaped watermelon on top. Make enough wands for each guest to have at least one.

2. Lay the popcorn and marshmallows flat on a piece of parchment paper.

3. Melt the pink candy melts according to the package directions. Transfer the melted candy coating to a quart-size plastic bag and cut a tiny piece off one of the bottom corners of the bag. Drizzle the candy coating over the popcorn and marshmallows, then immediately sprinkle the marshmallows with ¼ cup (37 g) of the pink sugar sprinkles. Let dry until set.

(CONTINUED)

4. Melt half of the white candy melts according to the package directions. Toss the Bugles in the melted candy coating until all are completely coated. Remove the Bugles and lay flat on a piece of parchment paper. Immediately sprinkle with the remaining ¼ cup (37 g) pink sugar sprinkles. Let dry until set.

5. To decorate the pink wafer cookies, melt the remaining half of white candy melts according to the package directions. Working with one wafer cookie at a time, dip one end a quarter of the way into the melted candy coating. Lay flat on a piece of parchment paper and immediately sprinkle the coated part with the pink pearl sprinkles. Let dry until set.

6. Put the pink M&M'S and pink jelly beans in round serving bowls and place the bowls on the board.

7. Fan the flower-shaped cookies around the bowl with the M&M'S in it.

8. Fan the pink pretzels around the bowl with the jelly beans in it.

9. Place the fruit skewers on the upper-left corner of the board and the Pocky sticks on the bottom right of the board.

10. Layer the wafer cookies down the right middle side of the board. Arrange the drizzled popcorn in the middle of the board and the drizzled marshmallows to the left of the popcorn.

11. Fill in the gaps on the board with the yogurt-covered raisins, fruit jellies, Bugles, and pink fish crackers.

12. Garnish the board with play princess crowns and a big frog gummy, if desired.

ENGAGEMENT
PARTY
BOARD

SERVES 12-14 PEOPLE

USE AN 8-INCH-ROUND (20 CM) × 7-INCH-HIGH (18 CM) WOODEN CAKE STAND
SET ON TOP OF A 15-INCH (38 CM) ROUND BOARD

The happy couple and their loved ones are sure to delight in the deliciousness of this elegant, tiered cheese-round cake that's adorned with blueberries, figs, and fresh herbs. Accompanied by a sophisticated selection of crackers, fruits, and nuts, it's a rustic yet chic twist on your typical engagement party cheese board or a creative alternative to a cheese lover's dream wedding cake. It's sure to leave a lasting impression on the couple and all their guests!

6-inch (15 cm) round of semisoft spreadable cheese (such as Brie, triple crème, or goat's milk)

4-inch (10 cm) round of semisoft spreadable cheese (such as Brie, triple crème, or goat's milk)

2-inch (5 cm) round of semisoft spreadable cheese (such as Brie, triple crème, or goat's milk)

3 bunches black concord grapes

¼ cup (38 g) blueberries

6 fresh figs, cut in half

⅓ cup (110 g) honey with honeycomb

24 round crackers

7 dried oranges

⅓ cup (45 g) dried apricots

2 dried hibiscus flowers

1 pear, thinly sliced

⅓ cup (50 g) candied pecans

⅓ cup (50 g) candied walnuts

6 large green olives

Fresh thyme sprigs and sage leaves, for garnishing

(CONTINUED)

NOTES

- I used Brie on the bottom, goat cheese in the middle, and truffled triple crème on top.
- Select your cheese rounds based on the number of people you're serving, your budget, and the selection at your local cheese shop or grocery store.
- Most grocery stores cut their cheese wheels, so ask someone at the cheese counter if they have whole cheese wheels for sale.

1. Stack the 6-inch (15 cm), 4-inch (10 cm), and 2-inch (5 cm) rounds of cheese on top of each other on the cake stand that fits on the larger round board.

2. Decorate the "cake" with some of the individual grapes, blueberries, and 2 fig halves.

3. Put the honey with honeycomb in a small serving bowl and place the bowl on the base board. Fan some of the round crackers around the honey bowl and the rest in another location on the base board.

4. Arrange the grape bunches in three different spots on the base board, followed by the dried oranges, dried apricots, and dried hibiscus flowers.

5. Add the sliced pear and fill in any gaps with the candied pecans and candied walnuts. Poke the green olives into little open crannies.

6. Garnish the "cake" and base board with sprigs of fresh thyme and sage.

TAKE ME OUT
TO THE
BALL GAME
BOARD

SERVES 6 PEOPLE | USE AN 18 × 12-INCH (46 × 30 CM) WOODEN TRAY WITH HANDLES

Hit it outta the ballpark with this snack board covered in a grand-slam selection of concession stand classics. Your little sluggers and all their baseball fanatic friends are sure to love the tasty hot dogs, peanuts, popcorn, and more. This is such a cute and creative way to serve snacks at a baseball-themed birthday party, World Series watch party, or end-of-season baseball team celebration.

6 frozen soft pretzels

15 White Fudge Dipped Oreo Thins Bites

1 small tube red cookie icing

6 mini hot dogs

6 mini hot dog buns

½ cup (120 ml) ketchup

½ cup (120 ml) mustard

3 to 4 cups (168 to 224 g) Cracker Jack popcorn mix

½ cup (120 g) Cheez Whiz, served warm

2 cups (112 g) whole peanuts in shells

12 medium-size whole kosher dill pickles

1. Bake the frozen pretzels according to the package directions.

2. Decorate the Oreos with the red cookie icing to look like baseballs. Set aside.

3. Heat the mini hot dogs and put them inside the mini buns. Place the hot dogs on the right side of the tray, along with squirt bottles filled with ketchup and mustard.

4. Fill a popcorn box with Cracker Jack popcorn overflowing out of it down the middle of the tray.

5. Line up the baked pretzels on the left side of the tray with the Cheez Whiz in a small serving bowl in front of them.

6. Arrange the peanuts along the Cracker Jack popcorn and the pickles next to the hot dogs.

7. Place some of the baseball Oreos on the popcorn box and the rest in a bowl to the side.

FOOTBALL
BOARD

SERVES 8-10 PEOPLE | USE A 20 × 16-INCH (51 × 41 CM) BOARD

We're a football-loving family! If we're not at the game, we're cheering on our favorite teams from our couch at home—and good snacks are essential. Get some skin in the game by creating this football-shaped snack board with a hefty selection of brown-colored snacks for the football shape and green-colored snacks for the grass around it. Score the extra point by garnishing with some goodies that are the colors of the team you're cheering for. So fun and festive!

35 Ritz Football Tailgate crackers

2 cups (220 g) football-shaped pretzels (such as Rold Gold brand)

1½ cups (90 g) sesame sticks

1 cup (150 g) whole roasted almonds

1 cup (150 g) dried figs

9 or 10 sweetened dried coconut strips

½ cup (120 g) pesto (store-bought or see recipe on page 159)

½ cup (120 ml) green goddess dressing

2 large bunches green grapes

2 cups (140 g) broccoli florets

1½ cups (115 g) sugar snap peas

½ cup (50 g) green olives

2 mini cucumbers, thinly sliced

20 asparagus tips

1½ cups (110 g) snow peas

½ cup (75 g) ready-to-eat shelled edamame

¼ cup (100 g) bread-and-butter pickle chips

2 green bell peppers, cut into strips

1. Arrange the brown-colored snacks into a football shape in the middle of the board. Line up the crackers as the center of the football, using a few crackers on either end to hold them in place. Then arrange the pretzels on either side of the crackers, the almonds on the outer sides of the pretzels, the sesame sticks on the outer sides of the almonds, and the figs on the outer sides of the sesame sticks.

2. Place the coconut strips to look like the white laces on top of a football.

3. Put the pesto and green goddess dressing in small bowls and place the bowls on opposite corners of the board.

4. Fill the remaining space around the football shape with the green snacks, starting with the green grapes and broccoli and working your way around each side with the sugar snap peas, green olives, cucumber slices, asparagus, snow peas, edamame, pickles, and green pepper slices.

GAME DAY
BOARD

SERVES 10 PEOPLE | USE A 29 × 15-INCH (74 × 38 CM) BOARD

Feed your home team with this epic spread of quick snacks and easy recipes for your next watch party. Whether you're watching a big football game or all the March Madness basketball action, this board of game-day greats is sure to be the winner. With chicken wings, bacon and pimento cheese–stuffed jalapeños, pigs in a blanket, and much more, there's something for every fan to cheer about. The snacks are what everyone really comes to a watch party for, right?

24 chicken wings in various flavors, store-bought or homemade, cooked

12 Bacon and Pimento Cheese–Stuffed Jalapeño Poppers (see recipe on page 151)

24 Pigs in a Blanket (see recipe on page 151)

12 frozen pretzel nugget bites, prepared according to package directions

1 bag (13.5 ounces, or 378 g) frozen onion rings, prepared according to package directions

2 cups (320 g) savory snack mix

2 cups (480 g) Chili con Queso Dip (see recipe on page 158)

1½ cups (360 g) guacamole (store-bought or see recipe on page 157)

½ cup (120 g) salsa (store-bought or see recipe on page 157)

½ cup (120 g) Cheez Whiz, warmed

¼ cup (60 ml) chunky blue cheese dressing

¼ cup (60 ml) ranch dressing

¼ cup (60 ml) ketchup

¼ cup (60 ml) mustard

4 celery ribs, cut into thirds

1 cup (110 g) fresh carrot chips

½ medium cucumber, thinly sliced

2 cups (120 g) blue corn scoop chips

2 cups (120 g) white corn scoop chips

1. Keep the wings, jalapeño poppers, pigs in a blanket, pretzel nuggets, and onion rings in a warm oven until ready to assemble the board.

2. Place the snack mix, chili con queso, and guacamole in large white serving bowls, the salsa and Cheez Whiz in medium serving bowls, the blue cheese and ranch dressings in small bowls, and the ketchup and mustard in mini bowls. Position all the bowls in various locations across the board.

3. Arrange the celery, carrot chips, and cucumber on the board.

4. Place the wings in groups of 8 near the blue cheese dressing and ranch dressing.

5. Place the pretzel nuggets near the Cheez Whiz, the pigs in a blanket near the ketchup and mustard, and the onion rings between the chili con queso and the guacamole.

6. Scatter the jalapeño poppers in various spots across the board.

7. Arrange the corn chips on opposite corners of the board.

NOTES
Place the chili con queso and Cheez Whiz in microwave-safe serving bowls so you can reheat them in the microwave as necessary.

MOVIE NIGHT
BOARD

SERVES 6-8 PEOPLE | USE AN 18 × 12-INCH (46 × 30 CM) WOODEN TRAY WITH HANDLES

Make movie night extra special with a showstopping board covered in popcorn and candy! Popcorn is the given, but how fun would it be to let each person pick their favorite movie-watching candy to add to the board? If you have guests joining in on the fun, ask them each to bring a small package of their favorite candy to contribute to the board. This board is perfect for family movie night, sleepovers, birthday parties, or a girls' night in. It's showtime!

½ cup (165 g) M&M'S (Peanut and Milk Chocolate)

½ cup (80 g) Skittles

4½ cups (72 g) popped popcorn

3½ cups (80 g) cheddar and caramel popcorn mix

14 red licorice twists

1 cup (165 g) peanut butter pretzel nuggets

1 cup (120 g) gummy bears

1 cup (165 g) mini peanut butter cups

1 cup (165 g) Hot Tamales candy

1 cup (120 g) Twizzlers Nibs

1 cup (165 g) Snickers Bites

¼ cup (120 g) Milk Duds

¼ cup (60 g) Dots candy

½ cup (80 g) Sour Patch Kids gummies

½ cup (60 g) Junior Mints

¼ cup (38 g) Raisinets

14 gummy worms

1. Put the M&M'S and Skittles in small star-shaped serving bowls and place the bowls on the tray.

2. Place the regular popcorn overflowing out of a popcorn box in the lower-left corner of the tray.

3. Spread the cheddar and caramel popcorn mix from the center to the upper-right corner of the tray.

4. Lay the red licorice in the upper-left corner of the tray.

5. Fill in the rest of the tray with the remaining candies and snacks.

DIM SUM
BOARD

SERVES 6-8 PEOPLE | USE AN 18-INCH (45 CM) LAZY SUSAN

Dim sum is all about sharing, so it's a given that we would need to have a good dim sum board up our sleeves for the perfect Saturday or Sunday with friends. The fun of dim sum is that there are no rules as to what you should eat when, so it's okay to have a little something sweet in between all the savory bites.

2 tablespoons (30 ml) chili garlic sauce

2 tablespoons (30 ml) dumpling or soy sauce

2 tablespoons (16 g) goji berries

5 green tea mochi balls

8 dried hibiscus flowers

6 almond cookies

8 dried persimmons

½ cup (60 g) dried banana chips

½ cup (75 g) sesame honey cashews

15 red and gold-wrapped chocolate coins

1 cup (60 g) Oriental rice cracker medley

½ cup (56 g) candied ginger

½ cup (65 g) Meiji Hello Panda chocolate crème-filled cookies

1 cup (60 g) mochi rice nuggets or bites

¼ cup (45 g) sesame sticks

½ cup (40 g) dried coconut strips

½ cup (40 g) rice bites with quinoa and cranberries (such as Trader Joe's Crunchy Nutty Rice Bites)

½ cup (50 g) wasabi peas

20 Strawberry Pocky biscuit sticks

20 Matcha Pocky biscuit sticks

8 frozen chicken and vegetable steamed dumplings

12 frozen chicken cilantro mini wontons

5 frozen vegetable spring rolls

1. Place 3 medium bowls on the lazy Susan that you will put the dumplings, wontons, and springs rolls in just before serving.

2. Put the chili garlic sauce, dumpling sauce, and goji berries in mini bowls and place these bowls next to each of the medium bowls on the lazy Susan.

3. Arrange the green tea mochi balls in the top center of the lazy Susan and garnish with the dried hibiscus flowers.

4. Fan out the almond cookies down the middle of the lazy Susan, followed by the dried persimmons.

5. On the left side of the lazy Susan, place the dried banana chips, sesame honey cashews, chocolate coins, Oriental rice cracker medley, candied ginger, Hello Panda cookies, and mochi rice nuggets.

6. On the right side of the lazy Susan, place the sesame sticks, dried coconut strips, rice bites, and wasabi peas.

7. Place the Strawberry Pocky sticks to the left of the mochi balls and the Matcha Pocky sticks to the right of the mochi balls.

8. Cook the dumplings, wontons, and spring rolls according to the package directions. Place in the medium bowls when ready to serve the board.

SEASONAL
AND
HOLIDAY
BOARDS

No decorations are needed with these creatively designed holiday boards, as they are masterpieces in themselves. Everyone will rave over how festive and delicious they are. They are almost too beautiful or too cute to eat . . . ALMOST! With coordinating colors and seasonal snacks coming together in very thoughtful arrangements, these boards are a great way to get into the spirit of any holiday season.

SPRINGTIME
BOARD

SERVES 6 PEOPLE ⟮ USE AN 18 × 11-INCH (46 × 28 CM) BOARD

This snack board is blooming with healthy and delicious snacks that are sure to put a smile on your face and a spring in your step. It is perfect for celebrating the first day of spring, the day you start planting your garden, or the passing of winter.

¼ cup (60 ml) ranch dressing

½ cup (120 g) garlic and herb spreadable cheese

¼ cup (60 g) vanilla-flavored yogurt

3 celery ribs

⅓ cup (55 g) candy-coated sunflower seeds

⅓ cup (50 g) multicolored yogurt-covered raisins

1 mandarin orange, peeled and segments separated

18 raspberries

2 large strawberries, stems removed and sliced

1 cup (110 g) baby carrots

1 cup (75 g) sugar snap peas

13 asparagus tips

2 cherry tomatoes

2 black olives

Butterfly-shaped crackers (such as Pepperidge Farm Golden Butter crackers)

1. Put the ranch dressing, spreadable cheese, and yogurt in small serving bowls and place the bowls on the board, with the spreadable cheese in the middle and placed higher than the other bowls.

2. Arrange the celery ribs coming down from the bottoms of the serving bowls to create stems. Fill the middle celery rib with the spreadable cheese.

3. Put the candy-coated sunflower seeds and the yogurt-covered raisins in small servings bowls and place the bowls near the bottom of the board on the left and right sides.

4. Alternate 9 of the orange segments and the raspberries around the middle bowl to create flower petals.

5. Lay the strawberry slices, points out, around the left bowl to create petals.

6. Place the baby carrots around the right bowl to create petals.

7. Lay the sugar snap peas and asparagus tips at the bottom of the board to look like grass.

8. Make 3 ladybugs with the cherry tomatoes and black olives: Cut the cherry tomatoes in half vertically and the black olives in half horizontally. Cut one of the black olive halves into tiny little pieces to lay on top of the tomato halves to look like ladybug spots. Place the remaining 3 black olive halves at the tops of 3 of the tomato halves, then arrange the little black dots on the tomato halves. Place 2 ladybugs on the filled celery stem and one in the grass.

9. Lay stacks of the butterfly crackers around the flowers on the board.

SUMMER FUN
BOARD

SERVES 10-12 PEOPLE | USE A 20-INCH (51 CM) ROUND BOARD

Splash into summer with this sweet day-at-the-beach board. Part beach ball, part beach bathing, this cute display of fruits and sweet treats is perfect for any summer celebration. Little touches, such as Teddy Grahams sunbathing on a beach with mini umbrellas shading them and sea-life gummies swimming in a blueberry ocean, make for a creative way to snack the summer days away.

½ cup (120 g) strawberry-flavored fruit dip

8 mandarin oranges, peeled and segments separated

3 cups (450 g) green grapes, cut in half lengthwise

3 medium bananas, peeled and thinly sliced

3 cups (510 g) halved strawberries

3 cups (500 g) pineapple chunks

3 cups (450 g) blueberries

2 small beach pails

1 cup (60 g) multicolored fish-shaped crackers

1 cup (110 g) round pretzels

12 graham crackers, broken in halves and quarters

6 rainbow sour candy chew strips

13 Teddy Grahams

3 umbrella toothpicks

2 watermelon gummies

4 Sixlets

7 Life Savers Gummies

8 fish and sea-creature gummies

1 shark gummy

1. Put the fruit dip in a small, white serving bowl and place the bowl in the lower middle of the board. Fan the orange segments, green grapes, banana slices, strawberries, and pineapple chunks around the white bowl to create a beach ball look, leaving the top open. Place all the blueberries at the open top to create the water that will lead up to the beach.

2. Place the 2 small buckets on either side of the board just above the blueberries. Fill one bucket with the fish crackers and the other with the round pretzels.

3. Fill the open space between the buckets and above the blueberries with layers of the graham crackers that are broken in halves and quarters. On 6 of the graham cracker quarters, lay a piece of rainbow candy to look like a beach towel, then place a Teddy Graham on top of each towel.

4. Open the umbrella toothpicks and poke the ends into the little holes of 3 of the graham crackers with the Teddy Grahams on them.

5. Place the watermelon gummies and the Sixlets next to the Teddy Grahams.

6. Stick Teddy Grahams into the Life Savers Gummies and arrange them in the blueberries, as if they are floating in the water. Scatter some of the fish and sea-creature gummies on top of the blueberries.

7. Place the gummy shark in the fruit dip.

FALL FEAST
BOARD

SERVES 10-12 PEOPLE | USE A 20-INCH (51CM) ROUND BOARD

It's fall, y'all! One of the most favored and flavored times of the year, the fall season is reason enough to gather people together and celebrate. This bountiful board of fall's finest flavors is perfect to make for a harvest party or Thanksgiving gathering. With a pumpkin cheese ball surrounded by an amazing assortment of sweet, savory, and spiced nibbles, this delicious board is sure to comfort everyone.

1 Pumpkin Cheese Ball (see recipe on page 152)

⅓ cup (80g) apple butter

⅓ cup (80ml) caramel dip

¼ cup (25g) pomegranate seeds

¼ cup (50g) candy corn

¼ cup (50g) pumpkin-shaped candies

¼ cup (40g) M&M'S Harvest Blend

4 celery rib leafy tops

4 mandarin oranges, peeled and left whole

10 Nutter Butter Acorns (see recipe on page 152)

6 maple leaf–shaped sandwich cookies

6 petite multicolored carrots, peeled and sliced in half lengthwise

15 cheddar cheese cracker cuts

12 honey wheat pretzel twists

½ large Honeycrisp apple, thinly sliced

7 whole pickled baby corn, drained and patted dry

3 pear halves, cored, and thinly sliced

2 thick slices pumpkin bread, cubed

20 to 25 vegetable tortilla chips

½ cup (65g) dried apricots

1 cup (60g) sweet potato crackers

1 cup (60g) beet crackers

1 orange bell pepper, cut into strips (reserve the stem for the pumpkin cheese ball)

12 dried figs

½ cup (75g) candied pecans

½ cup (60g) cheddar cheese cubes

1. Place the pumpkin cheese ball in the middle of the board. Put the apple butter, caramel dip, pomegranate seeds, candy corn, pumpkin-shaped candies, and M&M'S in small bowls and place the bowls across the board.

(CONTINUED)

2. Stick a small piece of celery leaf in the top of each mandarin orange to make them look like mini pumpkins and place them across the board.

3. Arrange the Nutter Butter acorns at the top of the board and fan the maple leaf–shaped cookies along the right edge of the board with the sliced carrots above them.

4. Fan the cheddar cheese cracker cuts along the upper-left edge of the board with the pretzel twists below them.

5. Arrange the apple slices and pickled baby corn on the left side of the board and place the sliced pear halves near the caramel dip.

6. Stack the pumpkin bread cubes from below the pumpkin cheese ball to the bottom of the board. Pile the tortilla chips to the top right of the pumpkin cheese ball.

7. Place the dried apricots, sweet potato crackers, beet crackers, and bell pepper slices on the bottom right of the board.

8. Fill in any gaps on the board with the dried figs, candied pecans, and cheddar cheese cubes.

WINTER WONDERLAND
BOARD

SERVES 6-8 PEOPLE ⟩ USE A 20 × 13-INCH (51 × 33 CM) BOARD WITH A LIP

Do you want to build a snowman? This adorable snack board is about the only snowman this mama gets excited about building. So, while the kids are out building Frosty, stay cozy inside making this board extra special with a snowman made with cheese rounds, a scrumptious selection of white-colored snacks for the snow, and a blueberry sky. This is such a great spread to enjoy during the winter months at a party with your friends or on a snowy day in with the family.

6-inch (15cm) round semisoft spreadable cheese (such as Brie, triple crème, or goat's milk)

4-inch (10cm) round semisoft spreadable cheese (such as Brie, triple crème, or goat's milk)

3-inch (7.5cm) round semisoft spreadable cheese (such as Brie, triple crème, or goat's milk)

7 blue crackers

19 Ritz Snowflake crackers, divided

32 ounces (907g) blueberries, divided

1 baby carrot

4 salami sticks, divided

¼ cup (60g) blueberry jam

7 white cheese star shapes (pre-cut or cut with a small cookie cutter)

¼ cup (80g) honey

2 cups (32g) popcorn

5 iced oatmeal cranberry dunkers (such as Trader Joe's Oatmeal Cranberry Dunkers with White Fudge Drizzle)

½ cup (75g) yogurt-covered raisins

1 cup (60g) mini rice crackers

⅓ cup (15g) mini snowman-shaped marshmallows

¾ cup (110g) sesame honey cashews

½ cup (40g) dried coconut strips

⅓ cup (45g) macadamia nuts

1. Place the 6-inch (15cm), 4-inch (10cm), and 3-inch (7.5cm) rounds of cheese in the middle of the board to look like a snowman.

2. For the snowman's hat, stack the blue crackers on one of the Ritz Snowflake crackers on top of the snowman's head and hold the pile in place with a blueberry.

3. Arrange blueberries for the snowman's eyes, mouth, and buttons and a baby carrot for the nose.

4. For the snowman's scarf, twist 2 of the salami sticks together and lay them over the space where the top two round cheeses connect, pressing the ends behind the snowman's neck and holding them in place with blueberries.

(CONTINUED)

5. For the snowman's arms, press the remaining 2 salami sticks into the sides of the cheese round in the center, letting them stick out, slightly tilted up.

6. Put the blueberry jam in a small serving bowl and place the bowl on the top right of the board. Fill the top third of the board with the remaining blueberries to create the blue sky. Scatter the cheese star shapes across the blueberries to make it look like stars in the sky.

7. Place the honey in a small serving bowl on the left side of the snowman in the middle of the board. Fan the remaining snowflake crackers on the right side of the bottom cheese round.

8. Arrange the popcorn across the bottom of the board and prop the cranberry dunkers just above the popcorn on the left side of the board, with the yogurt-covered raisins, mini rice crackers, and mini snowman-shaped marshmallows above them.

9. Fill in the right side of the board with the cashews, coconut strips, and macadamia nuts.

VALENTINE'S DAY
BOARD

SERVES 10+ PEOPLE | USE A 20-INCH (51 CM) ROUND BOARD

Serve up some love on Valentine's Day with this cute heart-shaped board that's been struck by Cupid's arrow. Layers of red-and-white goodies with a heart-shaped cracker arrow piercing through them makes for an adorable display that is equally delicious.

1 cup (240 g) vanilla fruit yogurt dip

20 pomegranate seeds

½ cup (75 g) white yogurt-covered almonds

¾ cup (90 g) raspberries

17 heart-shaped crackers (such as Valley Lahvosh Baking Co. Hearts Crackerbread, Original)

2 cups (240 g) white yogurt-covered pretzels

2 cups (120 g) beet crackers

2 cups (240 g) White Fudge Dipped Oreo Thins Bites

1 cups (160 g) red M&M'S

1 cups (40 g) mini marshmallows

32 ounces (907 g) strawberries, stems removed and cut in half

1. Put the the yogurt dip in a heart-shaped bowl and place the bowl in the center of the board. Create a heart shape with the pomegranate seeds in the middle of the yogurt.

2. Place a layer of the almonds, followed by the raspberries, around the heart-shaped bowl.

3. Make an arrow diagonally across the entire board with the heart-shaped crackers.

4. Continue to layer the remainder of the ingredients outward on the board in this order: white yogurt-covered pretzels, beet crackers, Oreo minis, red M&M'S, mini marshmallows, and strawberries.

MARDI GRAS
BOARD

SERVES 10+ PEOPLE ⎸ USE A 20-INCH (51 CM) ROUND BOARD

Let the good times roll with this Mardi Gras–themed board complete with a king cake, pralines, and even some beads for the luckiest of snackers. This spread proves you don't have to be in the Big Easy to make your own Fat Tuesday revelry.

1 store-bought king cake

¾ cup (120 g) purple, green, and yellow Skittles

¾ cup (120 g) purple, green, and yellow sour candy balls

1½ cups (180 g) purple, green, and yellow fruit-shaped gummies

24 gold-wrapped dark chocolate almond butter or peanut butter cups

12 mini powdered donuts

4 cups (240 g) purple, green, and yellow tortilla chips

Medium bunch of red grapes

Medium bunch of green grapes

2 cups (240 g) purple, green and yellow yogurt-covered pretzels

6 pecan pralines

9 ounces (252 g) peanut brittle

Purple, green, and gold beads, for decorating (optional)

1. Place the king cake in the center of the board, making sure you put the tiny plastic baby inside it first.

2. Put the Skittles and sour candy balls in small serving bowls and place the bowls on either side of the king cake.

3. Fan half the gummies around the Skittles bowl and the other half around the sour balls bowl.

4. Pile 12 of the gold-wrapped dark chocolate cups to the left of the fanned-out gummies at the top of the board and the other 12 to the right of the fanned-out gummies near the bottom of the board.

5. Line the powdered donuts on opposite sides of the king cake. Place half of the tortilla chips to the left of one row of donuts and the other half of chips to the right of the other row of donuts.

6. Arrange the red and green grapes on opposite sides of the board.

7. Pile half the pretzels to the right of the king cake and the other half to the left of the king cake.

8. Fill in the remaining gaps on the board with the pecan pralines and peanut brittle. Lay the beads on or near the board for decoration, if desired.

ST. PATRICK'S DAY
BOARD

SERVES 10+ PEOPLE | USE A 20-INCH (51 CM) ROUND BOARD

Get your green on with this shamrock-shaped board surrounded by the colors of the Irish flag. The luck of the Irish is sure to be with you and those you share this festive snack board with.

2 cups (300 g) green grapes, cut in half

¾ cup (180 g) pesto (store-bought or see recipe on page 159)

3 cups (225 g) snap peas

2 large green bell peppers, cut into strips

4 mini seedless Persian cucumbers, thinly sliced

5 cups (350 g) broccoli florets

30 round water crackers

30 orange cheddar cheese cracker cuts

6 mandarin oranges, peeled and segments separated

¾ cup (180 ml) ranch dressing, on the side, for dipping

1. Place a 12- to 14-inch (30 to 35 cm) shamrock-shaped board or a piece of parchment paper cut into a shamrock shape in the middle of a large board. Line the shamrock shape with the halved grapes and fill in the stem with grapes as well.

2. Put the pesto in a clear serving bowl in the center of the shamrock shape.

3. Lay the sugar snap peas in the left leaf of the shamrock, the green bell pepper strips in the top leaf of the shamrock, and the cucumber slices in the right leaf of the shamrock.

4. Fill the left side of the board with the broccoli florets. Place the water crackers above and below the shamrock in the center of the board. Line the right side of the board with the cheddar cheese cracker cuts.

5. Fill in the remaining space on the right side of the board with the orange segments.

6. Serve a bowl of ranch dressing on the side for dipping veggies.

EASTER CANDY
BOARD

SERVES 8-10 PEOPLE

USE A 10½ × 14-INCH (27 × 36 CM) EGG- OR OVAL-SHAPED WOODEN BOARD

This adorably simple Easter candy display, made with a colorful selection of pastel candies, pretzels, and marshmallows, would be perfect as the centerpiece to your Easter celebration table. Every bunny will be hopping their way over for a sweet treat.

9 yellow yogurt-covered pretzels

14 pink yogurt-covered pretzels

11 blue yogurt-covered pretzels

7 pink-coated Jordan almonds

11 green-coated Jordan almonds

10 white-coated Jordan almonds

8 purple bunny-shaped marshmallows

10 yellow bunny-shaped marshmallows

7 green bunny-shaped marshmallows

15 light blue M&M'S Peanut

17 pink M&M'S Peanut

13 orange jelly beans

20 purple jelly beans

26 yellow jelly beans

13 green jelly beans

1. Place the yellow pretzels in a row across the top quarter of the board, the pink pretzels in a row across the middle of the board, and the blue pretzels in a row across the lower quarter of the board.

2. Place the pink almonds just above the yellow pretzels, the green almonds just above the pink pretzels, and the white almonds just above the blue pretzels.

3. Place the purple marshmallows just below the yellow pretzels, the yellow marshmallows just below the pink pretzels, and the green marshmallows just below the blue pretzels.

4. Arrange the light blue M&M'S just above the green almonds and the pink M&M'S just above the white almonds.

5. Place the orange jelly beans above the row of pink almonds, leaving some exposed board above. Place the purple jelly beans between the purple marshmallows and blue M&M'S and the yellow jelly beans between the yellow marshmallows and the pink M&M'S. Place the green jelly beans below the green marshmallows, leaving some exposed board below.

AMERICAN FLAG
BOARD

SERVES 10+ PEOPLE | USE A 19 × 13-INCH (48 × 33 CM) SERVING TRAY

Shape red, white, and blue snacks into an American flag for the perfect patriotic addition to your Fourth of July, Memorial Day, or Labor Day celebration. Such a cute and clever way to show pride!

½ cup (75 g) raspberries

1 cup (150 g) Marcona almonds

2 cups (120 g) beet crackers

1 block (8 ounces, or 227 g) aged white cheddar, sliced into 10 strips

28 thin slices salami

12 ounces (336 g) Swiss cheese cubes

18 ounces (500 g) blueberries

1 medium red bell pepper, cut into strips

9 thick slices Havarti cheese, 6 slices cut into triangle shapes and 3 slices cut into 20 tiny stars with a small cookie cutter

1 cup (170 g) strawberry halves, stems removed

1 cup (60 g) mini rice crackers

1 cup (150 g) cherry tomatoes

1 cup (150 g) coconut cashews

¼ cup (38 g) dried cranberries

⅓ cup (80 ml) ranch dressing, for dipping

⅓ cup (80 g) yogurt fruit dip, for dipping

1. Place a diagonal row of raspberries in the bottom-left corner of the tray, followed by diagonal rows of almonds, beet crackers, white cheddar strips, salami, and Swiss cheese cubes.

2. Fill the upper-left corner of the tray with blueberries.

3. Finish the red-and-white stripes with the red bell pepper strips, Havarti cheese triangles, strawberries, mini rice crackers, cherry tomatoes, coconut cashews, and dried cranberries.

4. Place the Havarti stars on top of the blueberries.

5. Serve bowls of ranch dressing and yogurt dip alongside the tray.

PUMPKIN
BOARD

SERVES 10+ PEOPLE   USE A 20-INCH (51 CM) ROUND BOARD

Assemble a smiling jack-o'-lantern shape with a great variety of orange- and black-colored snacks, and it is sure to be a Halloween hit with all the little ghosts and goblins. Triangle-shaped cookie cutters are used to place the pumpkin's blackberry eyes and nose, while two big bunches of black grapes create the grin. Once the face is in place, you will fill it out with rows of orange snacks. A holiday hit!

3 triangle-shaped cookie cutters, for the eyes and nose

2 large bunches black Concord grapes

1½ cups (225 g) blackberries

¼ medium cucumber, thinly sliced

30 orange cheddar cheese cracker cuts

1½ cups (150 g) cheese crackers

2 cups (120 g) sweet potato crisps

1 bag (12 ounces, or 336 g) baby carrots

2 orange bell peppers, cut into strips

2 cups (32 g) orange cheddar popcorn

1½ mini cheese balls

2 cups (60 g) orange yogurt-covered pretzels

1 cup (30 g) seeded sweet potato crackers

1 cup (130 g) dried apricots

3 clementines, peeled and segments separated

Ranch dressing and hummus (store-bought or see recipe on page 156), on the side, for dipping

1. Place the cookie cutters on the board for the pumpkin's eyes and nose. Shape the black grapes into a grin. Fill the cookie cutters with blackberries.

2. Place the cucumber slices at the top of the board for the pumpkin's stem.

3. Fan the cheese slices down the middle of the board. Line the cheese crackers, sweet potato crisps, carrots, bell pepper slices, popcorn, cheese balls, pretzels, sweet potato crackers, apricots, and clementine segments out on both sides of the cheese slices and around the black foods until the board is completely covered. Tightly pack the orange foods at the edges of the board, so they stay in place if you transfer the board to another location to serve.

4. Carefully, lift the cookie cutters from the board, shaping the blackberries back into the triangle shapes, if necessary. You can always add more black and orange foods to fill in any gaps.

5. Serve bowls of ranch dressing and hummus on the side for dipping.

TURKEY
BOARD

SERVES 10+ PEOPLE | USE A 15-INCH (38 CM) ROUND BOARD

Gobble! Gobble! Here's a turkey that's almost too cute to eat. Almost! This turkey-shaped board is such a cute, festive, and, most importantly, tasty addition to your Thanksgiving celebration.

1 brown Bosc pear

26 orange cheddar cheese cracker cuts, divided

1 red bell pepper or red apple

Honey, for adhering items to the pear

1½ cups (225 g) candied pecans, divided

1 macadamia nut, cut in half

½ cup (60 g) dried cherries, divided

34 scalloped crackers

22 green grapes, cut in half lengthwise

22 red grapes, cut in half lengthwise

20 baby carrots

20 dried apricots

24 snow peas

1. Cut the pear in half, leaving the core on one side, and place the half without the core, cut side down, centered at the bottom of the board.

2. For the beak, cut a corner off one of the cheddar cracker cuts and place it upside down on the pear.

3. For the snood, cut a small piece of a red bell pepper or red apple and adhere it under the beak with a little honey.

4. For the feet, place 2 candied pecans at the bottom of the pear and adhere them with a little honey so they stick in place.

5. For the eyes, use the macadamia nut halves with a piece of dried cherry stuck to the center of the flat side of each one. Place them on the pear, flat side up, with a little honey to hold them in place.

6. From the pear, fan out all the snacks to look like turkey feathers: Place the scalloped crackers in 3 lines first, then add 2 lines of the remaining cheese cracker cuts between the lines of crackers.

7. Add the green grapes, cut sides down, between the crackers and cheese on the left side. Add the red grapes, cut sides down, between the crackers and cheese on the right side.

8. Place half of the remaining pecans between the cheese and crackers on the left side of the turkey and the other half between the cheese and crackers on the ride side of the turkey.

9. Fan the baby carrots out from the pear on the left side just below the line of crackers. Fan the dried apricots out from the pear on the right side just below the line of crackers on that side.

10. Place 12 snow peas so they're sticking out under the carrots on the left side and place the other 12 snow peas so they're sticking out under the dried apricots on the right side.

11. Add the remaining ¼ cup (30 g) dried cherries to each side of the bottom of the pear.

HANUKKAH
BOARD

SERVES 8-10 PEOPLE ⎪ USE A 20-INCH (51 CM) ROUND BOARD

Make Hanukkah extra special with this menorah-shaped board where everyone can build their own latkes and snack on the sweets that make it complete. Kids and adults alike will delight in this fun twist on the holiday classic.

10 to 12 latkes (store-bought or see recipe on page 153)

1 cup (150 g) blueberries

1½ cups (240 g) white yogurt-covered raisins

5 gold-wrapped dark chocolate almond butter cups, cut in half

2 sticks string cheese, each cut into fifths

9 large candy corn

⅔ cup (160 g) applesauce, for serving

⅔ cup (160 g) sour cream, for serving

1. Make or reheat the latkes. Use the latkes to create an upside-down *T* shape on the middle of the board to serve as the base for the menorah.

2. Use the blueberries to create 4 candleholders on either side of the base.

3. Fill in the space between each line of blueberries with the white yogurt-covered raisins.

4. Place the gold-wrapped chocolate halves, cut sides down, on the top of each line of blueberries. Top each chocolate with a piece of string cheese and then a candy corn to create the 9 lights.

5. Put the applesauce and sour cream in small serving bowls and place the bowls alongside the snack board.

SANTA
BOARD

SERVES 8 PEOPLE | USE A 20 × 13-INCH (51 × 33 CM) BOARD WITH A LIP

Ho! Ho! Ho! Santa never looked so good! Seriously simple and oh-so-cute, this Santa-shaped board will put you at the top of the nice list. Everyone will get such a kick out of your creativity as they enjoy this healthy addition to your holiday spread. And if your kiddos claim they don't like cauliflower, they just might try it when served as the big guy's beard, because Santa's watching, after all!

16 ounces (454 g) plain hummus (store-bought or see recipe on page 156)

1 can (6 ounces, or 168 g) large pitted black olives, divided

30 cherry tomatoes, divided

3 large red bell peppers, cut into strips, reserving ½ top of a pepper

1 container (8 ounces, or 227 g) fresh mini mozzarella balls, drained and patted dry

2 bags (12 ounces, or 336 g, each) cauliflower florets

18 club crackers

1 bag (12 ounces, or 336 g) broccoli florets

1. Evenly spread the hummus onto a round white plate with a lip around the edge. Place the plate in the center of the board.

2. Press 2 large black olives for Santa's eyes, a cherry tomato for his nose, and the ½ top of a bell pepper for his smile onto the hummus.

3. Layer the red bell pepper strips, starting from the top of the plate up to the top-right corner of the board to look like Santa's hat.

4. Add a line of mini mozzarella balls to the top edge of the plate and a small pile of mini mozzarella balls to decorate the top of Santa's hat.

5. Arrange the cauliflower for Santa's beard, mustache, and eyebrows.

6. Place the remaining black olives, except for one, at the bottom of the board, around the cauliflower beard to look like Santa's belt. Stack 3 club crackers at the very bottom center of the board with the remaining large black olive cut in half and the halves pressed together in the center of the top cracker to look like Santa's belt buckle.

7. Divide the remaining cherry tomatoes on either side of Santa's cauliflower beard, filling in from the olives up to the middle of the board.

8. Add the broccoli to the top left of the board and fan the club crackers along the right side of the board.

CANDY CANE
CAPRESE
BOARD

SERVES 8 PEOPLE / USE A 20 × 13-INCH (51 × 33 CM) BOARD WITH A LIP

Slices of fresh mozzarella and vine-ripened tomatoes layered in a candy cane shape make for a healthy and festive addition to your holiday spread. Serve with fresh basil, a balsamic glaze, and toasted baguette slices. Such a simple and savory way to impress your guests around Christmas.

1 package (16 ounces, or 454 g) fresh mozzarella cheese log, sliced ¼ inch (6 mm) thick into 13 slices

3 large tomatoes, sliced ¼ inch (6 mm) thick into 12 slices

9 fresh basil leaves

2 tablespoons (30 ml) balsamic glaze

Olive oil, to taste

Sea salt, to taste

1 large baguette, sliced and toasted

1. Start at the top end of the candy cane shape and alternate layering a slice of fresh mozzarella with a slice of tomato until you get a big candy cane shape.

2. Place fresh basil leaves around the board and a small serving bowl with the balsamic glaze.

3. Just before serving, drizzle the mozzarella and tomatoes with olive oil and sprinkle with sea salt. Serve with additional olive oil and sea salt, as well as the toasted baguette slices.

CHRISTMAS TREE
BOARD

SERVES 6-8 PEOPLE | USE A 20 × 15-INCH (51 × 38 CM) BOARD

Now, this is the kind of Christmas tree I really want to "decorate" and "take down." It's the perfect board to let the kids help with, as they will get such a thrill out of adding decorations, wrapping the cracker presents with strips of cheese, and putting the stars in the sky. Whether it be the appetizer for a holiday party, a snack on Christmas Eve, your contribution to the kids' classroom Christmas party, or just a fun activity to make for snack time with your family this holiday season, everyone is sure to enjoy it!

4 thick slices white cheese (Monterey Jack, white cheddar, Havarti, or provolone), cut into large stars with a cookie cutter

½ green pear, cored and thinly sliced vertically

20 cornichons

1 extra-large green bell pepper, cut into strips

3 cups (225 g) sugar snap peas

4 cups (280 g) broccoli florets

3 bunches green grapes

10 salami sticks

¼ cup (30 g) dried cranberries

11 raspberries

½ cup (30 g) red beet crackers

15 slices pepperoni or salami

13 red grapes

4 Triscuit crackers

1 thick slice white cheese, cut into small strips to create the ribbon look for cracker presents

1 cup (16 g) white cheddar cheese puffs

14 mini star-shaped cheese slices (precut or cut with a small cookie cutter)

Ranch dressing, on the side, for dipping

1. At the top center of the board, stack the 4 large cheese stars.

2. Starting from the star down, build the Christmas tree shape with all the green fruits and vegetables. Keeping it small at the top and building it out larger with each layer to the bottom of the tree shape, add the ingredients in this order: pear, cornichons, green bell pepper strips, sugar snap peas, broccoli florets, and green grapes.

3. Place the salami sticks as the trunk at the bottom center of the tree and tuck part of them under the green grapes.

(CONTINUED)

4. Use the red foods to create a garland look between each layer of green foods on the tree, placing them in this order: dried cranberries, raspberries, beet crackers, pepperoni slices, and red grapes.

5. Under the tree, create little presents with the Triscuit crackers and thin strips of white cheese for the ribbons. Under the presents, arrange some white cheddar cheese puffs to look like snow on the ground.

6 On either side above the tree, scatter the 14 mini cheese stars.

7. Serve a bowl of ranch dressing alongside the board for dipping veggies.

NEW YEAR'S EVE
BOARD

SERVES 10+ PEOPLE | USE A 20-INCH (51 CM) ROUND BOARD

Ring in the New Year in style with this stunning spread of sweet and savory snacks. Dressed in black and white with a cheese-round countdown clock in the middle, this board is a festive and formal affair without a lot of fuss. From the bow-tie fig cheese crackers to the dark chocolate star cookies, it's a spectacular spread that everyone is sure to enjoy as you welcome in the New Year.

6-inch (15cm) round semi-soft spreadable cheese (such as Brie, triple crème, or goat's milk)

1 small tube black cookie icing

8 to 10 black-and-white cookies

22 to 24 white cheese cracker cuts, divided

15 dark chocolate crème–filled rolled wafers

23 white round crackers, divided

1 log (5 ounces, or 140 g) goat cheese

4 tablespoons (60 g) blackberry jam, divided

½ cup (75 g) blackberries

1 large bunch black Concord grapes

1 wedge (6 ounces, or 168 g) Iberico cheese with a black rind

15 dark fruit and nut crackers

12 dark chocolate–covered star-shaped cookies

15 large pitted black olives

15 mini mozzarella cheese balls

8 small white spreadable cheese wedges (such as The Laughing Cow brand)

8 small black figs, cut in half lengthwise

¾ cup (120 g) dark chocolate–covered pecans or almonds

¼ cup (40 g) white yogurt–covered raisins

½ cup (30 g) coconut clusters

⅓ cup (45 g) Marcona almonds

½ cup (60 g) salt and pepper pistachios

1 cup (16 g) black-and-white popcorn (such as Popcorn Indiana Black & White Drizzlecorn)

1. Decorate the cheese round with the black icing to look like a clock with roman numerals. (You can also ask the cake decorator at your local grocery store to decorate it for you.) Place the cheese clock in the middle of the board.

(CONTINUED)

2. Layer the black-and-white cookies across the top of the board and fan the white cheese cracker cuts along the right edge of the board.

3. Place the rolled wafer cookies under the last cheese cracker cut and layer 15 of the white crackers along the bottom of the board leading up to the left side of the board.

4. Place the goat cheese log toward the bottom of the board. Top with 1 tablespoon (15 g) of the blackberry jam and put the fresh blackberries next to it. Put the remaining 3 tablespoons (45 g) blackberry jam in a small serving bowl and place the bowl on the right side of the board.

5. Arrange the black grapes on the left side of the board, with the Iberico cheese wedge just above it.

6. Fan the dark fruit and nut crackers around the top of the cheese clock and layer the star cookies between the round crackers and the black grapes.

7. Cut a slit in the top of each black olive, leaving the bottoms of the olives intact. Stuff each black olive with a mini mozzarella ball. Place the mozzarella-filled olives on the lower-right side of the cheese clock.

8. With the remaining 8 round crackers, place a small white spreadable cheese wedge on each one. Press together the pointed tips of 2 fig halves to look like black bow ties and place them on the wide part of each cheese wedge. Repeat with the remaining 14 fig halves. Place the bow-tie crackers in various locations across the board.

9. Fill in the remaining gaps on the board with the pecans, raisins, coconut clusters, almonds, pistachios, and popcorn.

BREAKFAST
AND
BRUNCH
BOARDS

From bagels to booze, I'm here to help you make the most important meal of the day the best meal of the day. These epic breakfast and brunch boards will get everyone up and at 'em, whether they're a morning person or not. These boards are built to bring everyone together and let them get creative with their meal or cocktail. Seeing the eagerness in everyone's eyes as they dig into these boards is what it's all about. This is a great way to start or end the day, especially if you're big on "brinner" (breakfast for dinner) like we are.

PANCAKE
BOARD

SERVES 6-8 PEOPLE | USE A 20 × 15-INCH (51 × 38 CM) BOARD

This pancake board is our absolute favorite for a slow weekend breakfast or, better yet, "brinner" (aka breakfast for dinner) on a weeknight. Everyone gets to top their pancakes just they way they like them. The kids get such a thrill out of spreading the butter themselves, and we have finally all learned how to pour our own syrup nice and slow, so our pancakes aren't soaking in it. We even have a little contest to see how creative we can get with fruit on top, so everyone's eager to grab and add a healthy serving of fruit to their plates. Served along with some crisp bacon and soft scrambled eggs, it's a meal that's sure to get even the sleepiest of heads out of bed. The excitement that brews as I'm building this board and the enjoyment that we all experience as we're eating off it are truly the best!

18 pancakes

10 slices bacon, cooked

8 eggs, scrambled

¾ cup (120 g) raspberries

¾ cup (130 g) sliced strawberries, stems removed

1 cup (150 g) blueberries

½ cup (80 g) chocolate chips

1 cup (10 g) whipped cream

2 bananas, peeled and sliced, reserving the peels for display

½ cup (1 stick, or 112 g) butter, sliced into small pats

¼ cup (65 g) peanut butter

¼ cup (60 g) chocolate hazelnut spread

1 bottle (3.4 ounces, or 95 ml) pure maple syrup

1. Keep the pancakes, bacon, and eggs warm in a low oven while you arrange everything else for the board.

2. Put the berries, chocolate chips, and whipped cream in small serving bowls and place the bowls on the right side of the board.

3. Place the bananas, fanned out on cleaned peels, and the butter on the right side of the board.

4. Put the peanut butter and chocolate spread in small jars and place the jars on the board.

5. Put the scrambled eggs in a serving dish and place the dish on the left side of the board. Layer the warm pancakes down the middle of the board and set the bacon on the left side of the board.

6. Heat the syrup, if desired, and add it to the board. Serve immediately while everything is warm.

BUILD-YOUR-OWN
PARFAIT
BOARD

SERVES 6-8 | USE AN 18 × 11-INCH (46 × 28 CM) BOARD

This board couldn't be easier to build and is quite possibly one of the most requested by my kids. Even my oldest, who claims he doesn't like yogurt or fruit, will eat several bowls of healthy parfait creations when I serve this board. He just gets into the action with everyone else, and it's amazing how much he loves it. And that example is exactly why we eat this way! Whether for an easy family breakfast on a Sunday morning or part of a brunch party with friends, this parfait board is sure to please even the pickiest of palates.

1½ cups (360 g) plain Greek yogurt

1½ cups (360 g) strawberry Greek yogurt

1½ cups (360 g) blueberry Greek yogurt

¼ cup (80 ml) honey with honeycomb

¼ cup (25 g) pomegranate seeds

¼ cup (40 g) Grape-Nuts cereal

¼ cup (27 g) slivered almonds

¼ cup (25 g) cacao nibs

¼ cup (25 g) multiseed ancient grains blend (such as Trader Joe's Super Seed & Ancient Grain Blend)

¼ cup (60 g) peanut butter or almond butter

1 cup (150 g) raspberries

1 cup (150 g) blackberries

¾ cup (120 g) blueberries

8 strawberries, with some sliced and some cut in half

1 banana, peeled and sliced

1 cup (150 g) fruit and nut granola

1 cup (150 g) granola clusters

1 cup (150 g) chocolate almond granola

¼ cup (20 g) toasted coconut chips

½ cup (60 g) chopped dried fruit

1. Place the yogurts in large (16-ounce, or 473 ml) Mason jars on 3 different areas of the board.

2. Put the honey with honeycomb in a serving bowl and place the bowl on the board.

3. Put the pomegranate seeds, Grape-Nuts, slivered almonds, cacao nibs, ancient grains blend, and peanut butter in small serving bowls and place the bowls across the board.

4. Add the berries and sliced banana to the board, followed by the granolas. Fill in any gaps with the toasted coconut chips and chopped dried fruit.

BAGEL
BOARD

SERVES 10   USE A 20 × 15-INCH (51 × 38 CM) BOARD

This bagel board is our absolute favorite! It's the ultimate brunch experience to enjoy with family and friends. It's so simple to put together, and everyone loves bagels! The bagels are definitely the stars of the spread, but it's all the fixings that make them shine. We literally sit for hours and build all sorts of delicious bagel creations while chatting and laughing the day away. From a plain bagel with plain cream cheese to an everything bagel with herbed cheese spread, sliced tomato, smoked salmon, capers, and a squeeze of lemon to a chocolate chip bagel with peanut butter, banana, and bacon—the options are exciting and endless. This board has seriously created some of our most cherished moments around our dining table.

10 regular-size bagels (variety of flavors)

5 mini bagels

1 cup (240 g) plain cream cheese

1 cup (240 g) blueberry cream cheese

1 cup (240 g) herbed cheese spread

¼ cup (60 g) peanut butter

¼ cup (60 g) chocolate hazelnut spread

2 to 3 tablespoons (40 to 60 g) honey

¼ cup (60 g) blueberry jam

¼ cup (60 g) apricot jam

¼ cup (35 g) capers

2 tablespoons (30 ml) crushed red pepper flakes

2 tablespoons (30 ml) everything bagel seasoning

1 medium cucumber, thinly sliced

8 ounces (227 g) smoked salmon, thinly sliced

4 sprigs fresh dill

1 large yellow tomato, thinly sliced

1 large red tomato, thinly sliced

1 avocado, peeled, pitted, and thinly sliced

½ small red onion, thinly sliced

3 or 4 radishes, thinly sliced

1 small lemon, cut into wedges

½ cup (1 stick, or 112 g) butter, sliced into small pats

¼ cup (35 g) blueberries

½ cup (75 g) raspberries

1 medium banana, peeled and thinly sliced

12 slices bacon, cooked

4 hard-boiled eggs, sliced

8 strawberries, cut in half

1. Layer the bagels down the middle of the board.

2. Put the cream cheese spreads in small bowls and place the bowls along the left edge of the board. Put the peanut butter, chocolate hazelnut spread, and honey in small bowls and place on the upper-right side of the board. Put the jams in small bowls and place the bowls on the bottom-right side of the board. Place the capers, crushed red pepper flakes, and everything bagel seasoning in really small bowls on the lower-left corner of the board.

3. Fan the cucumber slices in the upper-left corner of the board, then place the smoked salmon slices inside them. Garnish the salmon with the fresh dill.

(CONTINUED)

4. Layer the sliced tomatoes down the board between the cream cheese spreads and the bagels.

5. Place the sliced avocado, red onion, radishes, and lemon wedges on the bottom-left corner of the board.

6. Fan the butter pats around the jams on the bottom-right corner of the board. Add the blueberries and raspberries, followed by the sliced banana.

7. Stack the bacon in 2 spots on the right side of the board, with the sliced hard-boiled eggs in between.

8. Arrange the strawberries in the upper-right corner of the board.

NOTES

- You can slice the bagels in half before placing them on the board or set out a sharp knife for people to cut their own.

- I recommend buying the freshest bagels possible, as people will enjoy a really fresh baked bagel as is, though I always try to have the toaster out and handy if someone really wants to toast their bagel.

- You will find that people will take a half or even a quarter of one bagel to fix up one way and then a half or a quarter of a different bagel to fix up a completely different way. That's the beauty of this board—it allows everyone to taste and try several different bagel creations.

BLOODY MARY
BOARD

SERVES 6-8 PEOPLE | USE A 20 × 15-INCH (51 × 38 CM) BOARD

Whether guests like their Bloody Marys spicy, tangy, or mild, they will have a blast mixing up their own, and you will be freed from having to make them to order yourself. This board also serves as an appetizer with all the savory snacks. It's perfect to serve before a sweet brunch.

1 bottle (32 ounces, or 900 ml) Bloody Mary mix

1 bottle (2 ounces, or 56 ml) red hot sauce

1 bottle (4 ounces, or 113 ml) green hot sauce

7 petite carrots, peeled with 3 left whole and 4 cut in half lengthwise

2 celery ribs, cut in half and sliced into thin strips

4 mini red bell peppers, sliced into quarters lengthwise and seeded

6 pickled okra, 2 left whole and 4 sliced in half

6 whole pepperoncini peppers

¾ cup (90 g) olives with pimientos

¾ cup (90 g) pickled pearl onions

¾ cup (90 g) pickled vegetables

1 wedge (4 ounces, or 113 g) blue cheese

20 cheddar cheese cubes

20 pepper Jack cheese cubes

7 slices black forest or peppered bacon, cooked crisp

7 slices brioche toast

8 cocktail shrimp, cooked

¼ cup (60 ml) cocktail sauce

10 to 12 roasted shishito peppers

1 cup (150 g) mixed cherry tomatoes, cut in half

1 cup (50 g) toasted croutons

1 large lime, cut into wedges

1 large lemon, cut into wedges

2 tablespoons (30 ml) crushed red pepper flakes

2 tablespoons (30 ml) everything bagel seasoning (such as Trader Joe's brand)

2 bottles (12.7 ounces, or 375 ml) vodka

1. Pour the Bloody Mary mix into a large (16-ounce, or 473 ml) Mason jar or carafe and place on the upper-left side of the board. Place the bottles of hot sauce next to it.

2. Stick the sliced carrots, celery, red bell peppers, and pickled okra into mini jars and place the jars on the upper right corner of the board. Place the 3 whole carrots next to the jar with the sliced carrots and the 2 whole pickled okra next to the jar with the sliced pickled okra.

3. Add the pepperoncini peppers, olives, pickled onions, and pickled veggies to mini jars and place them along the bottom of the board.

(CONTINUED)

4. Place the blue cheese wedge, cheddar cheese cubes, and pepper Jack cheese cubes across the board.

5. Lay the bacon on the left side of the board and fan the brioche toasts up the right side of the board.

6. Place the shrimp on the lower-right side of the board with the cocktail sauce in a small bowl next to them.

7. Put the roasted shishito peppers in the middle of the board with the halved cherry tomatoes above them and the croutons below them.

8. Fill in any gaps with the lime and lemon wedges. Place the crushed red pepper flakes and everything bagel seasoning in mini bowls on the left side of the board.

9. Place the vodka alongside the board with some glasses filled with ice cubes for each person to make their own Bloody Mary as they snack off of the board.

NOTES

Plan for about 2 ounces (56 ml) of vodka and 4 ounces (112 ml) of Bloody Mary mix per cocktail.

MIMOSA
BOARD

SERVES 6-8 PEOPLE · USE AN 18-INCH (46 CM) LAZY SUSAN

Kick off your brunch get-together on a festive note by letting guests mix their own mimosas. With a great selection of juices and fruits, this board lets guests take their mimosa to the next level. We've had the best time with our friends and this board. We inspire each other to try different flavors and, believe it or not, one of the most preferred mixers is the green juice. Soooo good! Proves that mimosas are more than just orange juice and champagne. Cheers!

2 cups (480 ml) orange juice, chilled

2 cups (480 ml) Bolthouse Farms Berry Boost juice, chilled

2 cups (480 ml) Bolthouse Farms Green Goodness juice, chilled

2 bottles (750 ml each) champagne, chilled

¾ cup (110 g) blackberries

8 toothpicks, divided

¾ cup (110 g) blueberries

½ cup (88 g) diced mango

½ cup (50 g) pomegranate seeds

½ cup (82 g) diced pineapple plus 6 pineapple wedges, divided

½ cup (85 g) diced strawberries plus 5 whole strawberries, divided

½ cup (75 g) raspberries

1 cup (150 g) granola clusters

1 large orange, thinly sliced

8 mini cinnamon rolls

12 glazed donut holes

2 sprigs fresh mint

1. Pour the orange juice, berry juice, and green juice into small carafes and place the carafes on the board. Serve the champagne bottles on the board or keep them chilling in an ice bucket on the side.

2. Press 3 blackberries onto each of 4 toothpicks. Press 5 blueberries onto each of 4 toothpicks. Place the 8 blackberry and blueberry toothpicks next to the juice carafes on the lazy Susan.

3. Put the remaining blackberries and blueberries in small serving bowls. Also, put the diced mango, pomegranate seeds, diced pineapple, diced strawberries, and raspberries into individual serving bowls and place all the bowls around the edges of the lazy Susan.

4. Put the granola chunks in a bowl and place the bowl in the center of the lazy Susan. Surround the bowl of granola with the orange slices, pineapple wedges, whole strawberries, mini cinnamon rolls, and donut holes.

5. Use the fresh mint for garnish and also use it in a mimosa variation.

NOTES

• You might want to set out some ice for those who like their mimosas really cold.

• The ratios each person pours should depend on what they want to taste more—the juice or the champagne. Mix one-third juice and two-thirds champagne to satisfy those who desire booze over juice, reverse those quantities for a less boozy sip, and mix half juice and half champagne for middle-of-the-road mimosas.

MEAL
BOARDS

These are our meals—our go-to dinners and weekend lunches.
When I prepare a meal, more times than not, I will serve it on a
board. We've had great success eating as a family this way. Our kids
are engaged in the meal and actually eat the food. Everyone gets
so excited about what's on the board, and we all take such pride
in preparing our own plates. It's astonishing how much better the
kids eat when the meal is presented on a board compared to when
I pre-plate the same food for them. These boards are also great for
entertaining because they initiate conversation and inspire creativity,
making mealtime memorable.

PIZZA LOVERS
BOARD

SERVES 6-8 PEOPLE | USE A 14-INCH (35 CM) ROUND WOODEN PIZZA PADDLE

Friday night is done right with this board! It's almost as easy to build as it is to call in delivery, and it's sure to impress. With a mix of easy-to-prep, pizza-themed appetizers and some store-bought items that you can easily reheat, this board is any pizza lover's dream.

10 frozen mozzarella sticks

10 frozen pizza rolls

4 frozen garlic bread knots

20 frozen mini meatballs

½ cup (120 ml) pasta sauce

½ cup (120 ml) pizza sauce, for dipping

½ cup (120 ml) ranch dressing, for dipping

2 tablespoons (10 g) shredded Parmesan cheese

2 tablespoons (30 ml) crushed red pepper flakes

1 recipe Margherita Pizza Dip (see recipe on page 153)

10 gourmet pepperoni slices

¾ cup (123 g) pineapple chunks

8 baguette slices, cut ¼ inch (6 mm) thick and toasted

8 Mini Baguette Pizza Toasts (see recipe on page 153)

8 whole pepperoncinis

½ cup (60 g) whole black olives

6 fresh basil leaves, for garnishing

1. Bake the mozzarella sticks, pizza rolls, and garlic knots according to the package directions. Heat the mini meatballs according to the package directions and toss with the pasta sauce while still warm. Keep these items in a low oven until ready to place on the board.

2. When ready to assemble the board, put the pizza sauce and ranch dressing in small serving bowls and place the bowls next to each other on the pizza paddle.

3. Put the shredded Parmesan cheese and crushed red pepper flakes in mini serving bowls and place the bowls on the paddle.

4. Transfer the mini meatballs in pasta sauce to a serving bowl and place the bowl on the upper-right side of the paddle.

5. Place the margherita pizza dip on the lower-left portion of the paddle. Fan the pepperoni slices along the left edge of the pizza paddle with the pineapple chunks between them and the margherita pizza dip.

6. Place the toasted baguette slices near the top of the pizza dip and the garlic knots on the other side.

7. Along the top-left corner of the paddle, layer the mini baguette pizzas with the baked mozzarella cheese sticks to the right of them. Pile the pizza rolls on the right side of the paddle.

8. Fill in any gaps on the paddle with the pepperoncini and black olives. Chop one of the basil leaves and sprinkle over the pizza dip. Place the remaining 5 basil leaves around the board as garnish. Serve immediately.

BUILD-YOUR-OWN
TACO
BOARD

SERVES 8-10 PEOPLE / USE A 20 × 15-INCH (51 × 38 CM) BOARD

Now this is taco night, done right! What better way to bring people together than with a big board covered in colorful fillings for each person to fix their own tacos? With flour tortillas, hard shells, beef, chicken, shrimp, and an amazing selection of vegetables and fillings, there is truly something for everyone. And you can't have a taco bar without margaritas, so that's excuse enough to make this board. Taco 'bout fun and yum!

1 pound (454 g) ground beef

1 package (1 ounce, or 28 g) taco seasoning

1 pound (454 g) boneless, skinless chicken breast tenders

1 package (1 ounce, or 28 g) chicken taco seasoning

2 tablespoons (30 ml) cooking oil of choice, divided

1 pound (454 g) mini shrimp, peeled and deveined

1 package (1 ounce, or 28 g) shrimp taco seasoning

½ red bell pepper, thinly sliced and sautéed

½ orange bell pepper, thinly sliced and sautéed

½ yellow bell pepper, thinly sliced and sautéed

10 street taco–size flour tortillas

1½ cups (360 g) guacamole (store-bought or see recipe on page 157)

⅓ cup (40 g) shredded Monterey Jack and cheddar cheese

⅓ cup (40 g) crumbled cotija or queso fresco cheese

⅓ cup (5 g) chopped fresh cilantro

1 cup (240 g) pico de gallo (store-bought or see recipe on page 158)

1 cup (140 g) canned Mexican corn blend, drained

⅓ cup (50 g) chopped red onion

⅓ cup (80 g) salsa (store-bought or see recipe on page 157)

⅓ cup (80 g) sour cream

12 small taco shells

5 butter lettuce cups

1 cup (90 g) chopped purple cabbage

1 large jalapeño, thinly sliced

1 large lime, cut into wedges

1½ cups (360 g) refried beans

1. To make the ground beef, brown the meat in a large skillet over medium-high heat. Drain the fat, stir in the taco seasoning, and follow any additional instructions on the package.

2. To make the chicken tenders, toss the chicken in the chicken taco seasoning. Heat 1 tablespoon of the oil in a large skillet over medium heat. Add the chicken to the skillet and cook for 3 to 5 minutes per side, or until completely cooked through and no longer pink. Chop up the cooked chicken.

3. To make the shrimp, toss the shrimp in the shrimp taco seasoning. Heat the remaining 1 tablespoon (15 ml) oil in a large skillet over medium heat. Add the shrimp to the skillet and cook, stirring constantly, for 3 to 4 minutes, or just until the shrimp turn pink.

4. Keep the cooked beef, chicken, shrimp, and bell peppers warm in a low oven until ready to serve.

(CONTINUED)

5. Wrap the flour tortillas in foil and place in the oven to warm while you assemble the board.

6. Place 4 medium serving bowls on the board for the refried beans, beef, chicken, and shrimp. You will fill these bowls with the warm foods just before serving the board.

7. Put the guacamole, shredded cheese, cotija crumbles, chopped cilantro, pico de gallo, Mexican corn, chopped red onion, salsa, and sour cream in serving bowls and place the bowls across the board.

8. Fan the taco shells down the middle of the board.

9. Place the lettuce cups, chopped cabbage, sliced jalapeño, and lime wedges in open spaces on the board.

10. Heat the refried beans and spoon them into one of the empty serving bowls already on the board or heat them directly in the serving bowl if it's microwave or oven safe.

11. Place the warm sautéed bell peppers on the board, then fill the remaining empty serving bowls on the board with the beef, chicken, and shrimp.

12. Arrange the warm flour tortillas around the top of the board near the refried beans.

MEDITERRANEAN MEZZE
BOARD

SERVES 6-8 PEOPLE | USE A 20 × 13-INCH (51 × 33 CM) BOARD WITH A LIP

This fresh and flavorful board loaded with Mediterranean favorites is perfect for snacking and entertaining. Our whole family eats well when there's hummus and lots of pita and vegetables to dip in it. Along with some heartier bites, such as dolmas and falafel, this mezze board makes for a healthy meal that comes together quickly.

16 ounces (454 g) hummus (store-bought or see recipe on page 156)

6 frozen falafel, baked according to package directions

6 frozen spanakopita, baked according to package directions

¾ cup (180 g) tabbouleh

⅓ cup (80 ml) tzatziki sauce

⅓ cup (80 ml) Lebanese garlic sauce (such as Trader Joe's Garlic Spread-Dip)

⅓ cup (40 g) marinated olive medley

1 medium cucumber, half cut into slices and half cut into chunks

8 medley cherry tomatoes, cut in half

¼ small red onion, sliced

10 dolmas (stuffed grape leaves)

½ cup (60 g) pickled vegetables

3 rounds of pita bread, cut into quarters

8 Medjool dates, tops sliced open and pits removed

⅓ cup (80 g) prepared creamy labneh or thick strained Greek yogurt

6 marinated artichoke halves

6 small squares baklava

¼ cup (30 g) pistachios

¼ cup (35 g) candied walnuts

1 block (8 ounces, or 227 g) feta cheese

⅓ cup (80 g) canned chickpeas, rinsed and drained

1 lemon, cut into wedges

Olive oil, for drizzling (optional)

1 tablespoon (6 g) minced roasted garlic, for garnishing (optional)

1 tablespoon (4 g) chopped fresh parsley, for garnishing (optional)

1. Evenly spread the hummus onto a plate with a slight rim. Place the plate in the middle of the board.

2. Keep the falafel and spanakopita warm in a low oven until you are ready to serve the board.

3. Put the tabbouleh, tzatziki, garlic sauce, and olives in small serving bowls and place the bowls across the board.

4. Fan the cucumber slices around the bottom portion of the hummus plate. Toss the cucumber chunks, reserving a chunk for garnishing later, in a small bowl with the halved cherry tomatoes and sliced red onion. Spoon the cucumber, tomato, and red onion mixture onto the board to the left of the hummus plate.

5. Place the dolmas on the right side of the hummus plate with the pickled vegetables below them.

(CONTINUED)

6. Stack the pita bread quarters along the bottom-right edge of the board.

7. Fill each date with a heaping teaspoon of labneh and place the stuffed dates on the bottom-left corner of the board.

8. Fan the artichoke halves along the top-right corner of the board and the baklava along the top-left corner of the board, with the pistachios and candied walnuts below the baklava.

9. Crumble the feta into large chunks just above the dolmas. Take a few chunks of the feta and sprinkle them over the cucumber, tomato, and red onion mixture.

10. Place the chickpeas on the bottom left of the board near the garlic sauce and labneh-stuffed dates. Arrange the lemon wedges around the edges of the board.

11. Add the warm spanakopita to the top center of the board and the warm falafel to the bottom center of the board.

12. Drizzle olive oil, if desired, over the hummus and the cucumber, tomato, and red onion mixture.

13. Finely dice the reserved cucumber chunk and use it to garnish the tzatziki sauce. Garnish the garlic sauce with the minced roasted garlic, if desired, and the hummus with the parsley, if desired.

GRILLED CHEESE
BOARD

SERVES 6-8 PEOPLE | USE A 15-INCH (38 CM) ROUND BOARD

Make your guests melt with this grilled cheese board that's the ultimate in delicious comfort. Kids and grown-ups alike will love this board that offers everything from a classic grilled cheese to a more creative combo of Brie and fig jam. The possibilities are endless, though, when it comes to the varieties of grilled cheeses you could make to put on this board. And don't forget the tomato sauce in the middle for dipping—you can't have grilled cheese without tomato "soup!" It hits all the right buttons for family-friendly entertaining: fun, delicious, easy, and comforting.

1 jar (24 ounces, 672 g) tomato sauce with basil, for dipping

3 Classic Grilled Cheese Sandwiches (see recipe on page 154), each cut into 4 long strips

2 Bacon Cheddar Grilled Cheese Sandwiches (see recipe on page 154), each cut into quarters

8 Brie and Fig Jam Grilled Cheese Sandwiches (see recipe on page 154)

¼ cup (60 ml) ranch dressing

¼ cup (60 g) apple butter

1 large bunch green grapes

2 cups (60 g) wavy potato chips

2 small pears, thinly sliced

15 bread-and-butter pickle chips

Olive oil, for drizzling

Parmesan cheese, for garnishing (optional)

Fresh basil, for garnishing (optional)

1. Heat the tomato sauce in a pan over low heat.

2. Place a soup bowl in the middle of the board. Arrange the grilled cheese sandwiches in three separate areas around the soup bowl. Put the ranch dressing and apple butter in small bowls and place the bowls between the groups of grilled cheese sandwiches.

3. Arrange the grapes, potato chips, sliced pears, and pickles between the groups of sandwiches.

4. Pour the heated tomato sauce into the bowl in the center of the board. Drizzle the tomato sauce with olive oil and a sprinkle of Parmesan cheese (if using) and fresh basil (if using).

BUILD-YOUR-OWN
COBB SALAD
BOARD

SERVES 6 PEOPLE | USE AN 18-INCH (46 CM) LAZY SUSAN

This Cobb salad board is the reason our kids eat and enjoy salads so much. It's one of our go-to weeknight dinners because everyone eats so well when I serve it. The kids beg for it on the regular. They love creating their own Cobb salads with all the tasty topping options.

5 cups (150 g) chopped lettuce mix

½ cup (60 g) shredded cheddar and Monterey Jack cheese

½ cup (40 g) crumbled cooked bacon (about 5 slices)

½ cup (60 g) blue cheese crumbles

½ cup (72 g) diced avocado

½ cup (120 ml) chunky blue cheese dressing

½ cup (120 ml) ranch dressing

1 cup (150 g) glazed pecans

4 hard-boiled eggs, sliced

1 pound (454 g) boneless, skinless chicken breast, grilled and cut into bite-size chunks

1 cup (150 g) cherry tomatoes, halved

½ medium red onion, thinly sliced

1 cup (50 g) croutons

1. Place the lettuce mix in the middle of the lazy Susan, leaving space all around it for the toppings.

2. Put the shredded cheese, crumbled bacon, blue cheese crumbles, and diced avocado in serving bowls and place the bowls next to each other on the left side of the lettuce mix.

3. Place the blue cheese and ranch dressings in small jars on either side of the bowls of toppings.

4. On the right side of the lettuce mix, place the glazed pecans, sliced hard-boiled eggs, chopped grilled chicken, cherry tomato halves, sliced red onion, and croutons.

BUILD-YOUR-OWN
SANDWICH
BOARD

SERVES 10 PEOPLE | USE A 20 × 16-INCH (51 × 41 CM) BOARD

A simple build-your-own sandwich board is the perfect fuss-free way to feed a hungry crowd. It's covered with a great assortment of fillings so that each person can build their best sandwich. The excitement on people's faces when they approach the board is pretty awesome. You can just see their eyes grow big and a smile of concentration light their faces as they choose their bread, meats, cheeses, veggies, and spreads. The combinations are endless! This is a great idea for game day, a birthday party, holidays, or any casual get-together. I just put out plates and let everyone start building their sandwiches when they're ready. It's an easy, awesome meal that everyone is sure to enjoy.

6 slices deli-style sourdough or Italian white bread

6 slices deli-style multigrain or three-seed bread

2 pretzel baguettes

4 small ciabatta rolls

¼ cup (44 g) whole-grain mustard

¼ cup (60 g) mayonnaise

¼ cup (44 g) yellow mustard

8 slices pepper Jack cheese

6 slices American cheese

6 slices provolone cheese

8 slices turkey

8 slices roast beef

8 slices ham

8 slices salami

6 slices thick-cut bacon, cooked

6 lettuce leaves

½ red onion, thinly sliced

½ avocado, thinly sliced

1 large tomato, thinly sliced

10 bread-and-butter pickle chips

6 dill pickle flats

1. Arrange the breads along the top of the board.

2. Place the whole-grain mustard, mayonnaise, and yellow mustard in mini serving dishes on the left side of the board.

3. Diagonally layer the cheeses under the bread, followed by the sliced meats. Lay the bacon under the sliced meats.

4. Place the lettuce, onion, avocado, tomatoes, pickle chips, and pickle flats along the bottom of the board and to fill in any gaps in the middle of the board.

BARBECUE
BOARD

SERVES 6-8 / USE A 20 × 16-INCH (51 × 41 CM) BOARD

Wow your crowd with this finger-licking spread of meats, sides, and sauces. Smoke your own meats and make your own sides or, better yet, pick up the meats and sides from your favorite barbecue joint to build this board. Add some grilled corn, pickles, pickled jalapeños, watermelon, corn muffins, and, of course, white bread, and you're done! This board is a celebration in itself and such a great way to enjoy food and time with great friends.

1 cup (240 g) baked beans

1 cup (140 g) macaroni and cheese

1 cup (90 g) coleslaw

⅓ cup (80 ml) traditional barbecue sauce

⅓ cup (80 ml) mustard-based barbecue sauce

⅓ cup (80 ml) sweet and spicy barbecue sauce

5 slices soft white bread

8 mini corn muffins

5 spareribs

2 smoked sausage links, sliced

½ pound (227 g) smoked brisket, sliced

½ pound (227 g) smoked chicken or turkey, sliced

½ pound (227 g) smoked pulled pork

3 ears grilled corn, cut in half

8 small watermelon wedges, with rinds

½ cup (120 g) bread-and-butter pickle chips

¼ cup (40 g) sliced red onion

½ cup (65 g) pickled jalapeños

1. Order the barbecue and sides from your favorite local barbecue restaurant or from the grocery store deli/smokehouse.

2. Begin by placing the baked beans, macaroni and cheese, and coleslaw in serving bowls and place the bowls across the board.

3. Put the barbecue sauces in small serving bowls and place the bowls across the board.

4. Fan the white bread on the top-right corner of the board and pile the mini corn muffins on the bottom-left corner of the board.

5. Arrange the smoked meats down the board: ribs, one of the sausage links, sliced brisket, smoked chicken or turkey, the remaining sausage link, and pulled pork.

6. Place the watermelon wedges on the right side of the board. Add the pickles, sliced red onion, and pickled jalapeños to the remaining space on the board. Serve immediately.

DESSERT
BOARDS

Dessert boards are the way to go when treating a crowd to something sweet. These spectacularly sweet boards can be mostly prepped in advance, making it easy to quickly serve dessert when you're ready. They are the perfect ending to any dinner party or the main event at a special celebration. Most of these boards are build-your-own—an experience to remember. We can all agree that building our own s'mores or ice cream sundaes is pretty special!

S'MORES
BOARD

It's sure to be a sweet night when a s'mores board is in the plans! This board is our absolute favorite go-to dessert for family night or a summer night around the firepit with friends. From the classic (graham crackers, chocolate bar, and roasted marshmallow) to the King (graham crackers, chocolate peanut butter cup, banana slices, and roasted marshmallow), this board is sure to please everyone as they indulge in this interactive s'mores experience.

1 recipe S'mores Snack Mix (see recipe on page 155)

¾ cup (190 g) peanut butter

12 s'more-size marshmallows

5 whole graham crackers, broken in half

5 whole chocolate graham crackers, broken in half

3 Hershey's Milk Chocolate bars (1.55 ounces, or 43 g), broken in half

10 round fudge-striped cookies

14 pretzel chips

8 to 10 chewy chocolate chip cookies

8 gourmet chocolate squares

10 round chocolate marshmallows

1 Hershey's Gold Carmelized Crème bar (1.4 ounces, or 40 g), broken into pieces of 2 squares

8 peanut butter cups

1 Hershey's Cookies 'n' Crème bar (1.55 ounces, or 43 g), broken into pieces of 2 squares

5 strawberries, stems removed and sliced

1 recipe S'mores Dip (see recipe on page 155)

1 cup (40 g) graham cracker sticks

1 banana, peeled and sliced

1. Put the s'mores snack mix and peanut butter in serving bowls and place the bowls on the board.

2. Place the s'more-size marshmallows on the middle of the board.

3. Fan the regular graham cracker halves on the upper-right corner and the chocolate graham cracker halves on the lower-left corner. Set the Hershey's Milk Chocolate bars on the top middle of the board.

4. Place the cookies on the left side of the board with the pretzel chips to the right of them. Line the chocolate chip cookies down the lower-right corner.

5. Fan the gourmet chocolate squares around the s'mores snack mix bowl on the right edge of the board. Stack the round chocolate marshmallows under the chocolate squares

6. Place the Hershey's Gold bar pieces, peanut butter cups, and Cookies 'n' Crème bar pieces on the bottom of the board along with the strawberry slices.

7. Place the s'mores dip on the upper-left corner with the graham sticks around it for dipping.

8. Arrange the sliced banana in the upper-right corner of the board.

DECORATE-YOUR-OWN
CUPCAKE
BOARD

SERVES 12+ PEOPLE | USE A 29 × 15-INCH (74 × 38 CM) BOARD AND A MINI CAKE STAND

The kids go crazy over this board. It's so fun watching their excitement as they approach the board in anticipation of what their cupcake is going to look and taste like. It's such a great way to entertain them and serve dessert at the same time. Whether it's a birthday party, a sleepover, or a holiday-themed get-together with friends, this is an easy way to make the occasion more memorable for all!

20 regular-size cupcakes (vanilla, chocolate, and/or strawberry)

15 mini cupcakes (vanilla, chocolate, and/or strawberry)

8 silicone cupcakes liners, to hold toppings

½ cup (14 g) Froot Loops cereal

½ cup (82 g) colorful mini chocolate chips

½ cup (80 g) mini peanut butter cups

½ cup (80 g) jelly beans

½ cup (80 g) M&M'S Minis

½ cup (20 g) mini marshmallows

½ cup (75 g) heart-shaped sprinkles

½ cup (50 g) mini gummy bears

12 assorted mini sprinkles shakers (1 ounces, or 28 g, each)

14 Oreo Mini cookies

12 flower-shaped icing decorations

1 bag (16 ounces, or 454 g) vanilla frosting

1 bag (16 ounces, or 454 g) chocolate frosting

1 bag (16 ounces, or 454 g) strawberry frosting

1. Bake your favorite cupcake recipe(s) from scratch or use a box mix, making both regular-size and mini ones, and using your desired cupcake liners. Let the cupcakes cool completely before setting them on the board to decorate. Cupcakes can be baked days or weeks in advance and stored, tightly covered, in the freezer. To defrost the cupcakes, set them out, loosely covered, at room temperature. Once completely defrosted, they can be decorated.

2. Place the mini cake stand in the center of the board. Top the cake stand with 12 to 14 mini cupcakes and place the remaining mini cupcakes next to it.

3. Arrange the regular-size cupcakes on the board above and below the cake stand.

4. Use the 8 silicone cupcake liners to hold the following cupcake toppings: cereal, mini chocolate chips, mini peanut butter cups, jelly beans, M&M'S, mini marshmallows, heart-shaped sprinkles, and mini gummy bears. Place 4 topping-filled cupcake liners on the left side of the cake stand and 4 topping-filled cupcake liners on the right side of the cake stand.

5. Place 6 of the mini sprinkles shakers on the left side of the board and 6 on the right side of the board.

6. Arrange the Oreo cookies on one side of the board and the flower-shaped icing decorations on the other side.

7. Place the frosting-filled pastry bags fitted with star tips in separate locations on the board along with mini spatulas for spreading frosting onto the cupcakes, if desired.

8. Give each person a 5-inch (12.5 cm) pie pan or plate with a rim to set under their cupcakes as they decorate them, so it can collect any toppings or decorations that might fall off.

CHOCOLATE FONDUE
BOARD

SERVES 8-10 PEOPLE | USE AN 18-INCH (46 CM) LAZY SUSAN

This chocolate fondue board is one of the easiest and most enjoyable desserts I make when we have guests over for dinner. I love how interactive it is. Our friends and family go crazy over all the delicious dippers as they work their way around the board. The delectable melted chocolate takes each dipper to the next level. It's so fun to see which combo is the favorite. I'm always pleasantly surprised when most people reach back in for the figs and Rice Krispies Treats. Nontraditional fondue dippers for the win!

1 cup (165 g) chocolate fondue melting wafers (such as ChocoMaker Dark Fountain Formula)

10 chocolate chip cookie dippers (such as Trader Joe's Chocolate Chip Cookie Dunkers)

2 bananas, peeled and cut into thick slices

25 dried apricots

12 dried figs

20 cubes pound cake

16 chocolate-filled rolled wafer cookies

18 regular-size marshmallows

10 large strawberries

8 to 10 dried orange slices

8 to 10 coconut macaroons

16 brownie squares

12 to 14 Rice Krispies Treats Mini Squares

16 pretzel sticks

1. Place a mini microwave-safe fondue pot in the center of the lazy Susan with the chocolate fondue melting wafers in it. Wait to melt the wafers until the board is assembled and you're ready to serve the fondue.

2. Place all the dippers, clockwise, around the fondue pot, starting from the top: chocolate chip cookies, bananas, apricots, figs, pound cake, wafer cookies, marshmallows, strawberries, orange slices, macaroons, brownies, Rice Krispies Treats, and pretzel sticks.

3. Melt the chocolate wafers according to the package directions. Set the fondue pot back in the center of the board. Light the flame underneath the pot to keep it warm.

BUILD-YOUR-OWN
SUNDAE
BOARD

SERVES 12+ PEOPLE ⟩ USE A 20 × 15-INCH (51 × 38 CM) BOARD

This is definitely the "coolest" board I've created! I first made it for my mom's birthday several years ago because she loves ice cream sundaes. We even put candles in the cartons of ice cream when we sang "Happy Birthday" to her. It was a sweet celebration and one that we've recreated several times for last-day-of-school celebrations, birthday parties, and backyard barbecues! Everyone always has so much fun building and eating their own sundaes with this epic assortment of cones, ice creams, and toppings to choose from.

1 cup (240 ml) fudge topping

1 cup (240 ml) caramel topping

1 cup (240 ml) strawberry topping

1 cup (240 ml) marshmallow topping

18 sugar cones

8 waffle bowls

20 mini cake cones

12 chocolate-filled wafer cookies

18 maraschino cherries

10 Oreo Thins cookies

8 to 10 chewy chocolate chunk cookies

8 large cake cones

½ cup (80 g) toffee bits

½ cup (80 g) mini chocolate chips

½ cup (20 g) marshmallow bits

½ cup (75 g) chopped nut mix

½ cup (50 g) mini gummy bears

½ cup (75 g) sprinkles

½ cup (80 g) M&M'S Minis

½ cup (80 g) colorful chocolate chips

½ cup (70 g) Nestlé Buncha Crunch candy

½ cup (80 g) mini peanut butter cups

½ cup (80 g) chopped Snickers candy bars

½ cup (80 g) jelly beans

½ cup (80 g) Reese's Pieces

½ cup (70 g) Nerds candy

1 banana, peeled and sliced

8 strawberries, stems removed and sliced

2 cups (150 g) whipped topping

1 pint (450 g) vanilla ice cream

1 pint (450 g) chocolate ice cream

1 pint (450 g) strawberry ice cream

1 pint (450 g) mint chocolate chip ice cream

1. Place a 12 × 7 × 3-inch (30.5 × 18 × 7.5cm) galvanized bucket in the center of the board.

2. Transfer the fudge, caramel, strawberry, and marshmallow toppings to squirt bottles, if desired, and place the bottles just above the galvanized bucket.

3. Place the sugar cones just below the galvanized bucket, the waffles bowls on the bottom-right corner of the board, and the mini cake cones at the top middle of the board.

4. Put the wafer cookies in a small jar on the top-left corner and the maraschino cherries in a small jar on the top-right corner of the board

(CONTINUED)

5. Layer the Oreo cookies next to the cherries on the top-right corner and fan the chewy chocolate chunk cookies along the bottom-left edge of the board.

6. Fill the 8 large cake cones with the following toppings: toffee bits, mini chocolate chips, marshmallow bits, chopped nut mix, mini gummy bears, sprinkles, M&M'S, and mini chocolate chips. Stand 4 cones on either side of the galvanized bucket.

7. Fill 6 small (4-ounce, or 118 ml) Mason jars with the following toppings: Nestlé Buncha Crunch candy, mini peanut butter cups, chopped Snickers candy bars, jelly beans, Reese's Pieces, and Nerds. Place 3 jars along the far-left edge of the board and 3 jars along the far-right edge.

8. Arrange the sliced banana by the wafer cookies on the top-left corner and the sliced strawberries by the waffle bowls on the bottom-right corner of the board.

9. Serve the whipped topping in a pastry bag with a decorative tip; alternatively, place the whipped topping in a serving bowl and place the bowl on the bottom of the board.

10. When ready to serve the board, place the 4 pints of ice cream in the galvanized bucket and put ice around them to keep them frozen while guests are building their ice cream sundaes.

RECIPES

OATMEAL CHOCOLATE CHIP BITES

(MAKES 20)

2½ cups (200 g) quick-cooking oats

1 cup (260 g) peanut butter

⅓ cup (110 g) honey

½ cup (85 g) chocolate chips

1. In a large bowl, mix together the oats, peanut butter, and honey until well combined.

2. Fold in the chocolate chips so they are well distributed.

3. Roll the mixture into 2 tablespoon-size (30 g) balls for a total of 20 smooth balls.

4. Refrigerate any leftover bites.

SNACK MIX

(MAKES 1 CUP, OR 140 G)

⅓ cup (30 g) mini pretzels

⅓ cup (50 g) peanuts

⅓ cup (56 g) M&M'S

1. In a medium bowl, combine the pretzels, peanuts, and M&M'S.

BIRTHDAY SNACK MIX

(MAKES 7 CUPS, OR 400 G)

4 cups (108 g) Rice Chex cereal

1 cup (100 g) Snyder's of Hanover Itty Bitty Minis pretzels

½ cup (70 g) dry-roasted peanuts

1 package (16 ounces, or 454 g) vanilla candy coating (such as CandiQuik brand)

1 container (5.25 ounces, or 147 g) rainbow sprinkles, divided

1 container (1.3 ounces, or 36 g) pastel confetti sprinkles

1 cup (28 g) Froot Loops cereal

18 Birthday Hat Bugles (see recipe below)

1. Line a large baking sheet with parchment paper. Set aside.

2. In a large bowl, combine the Chex cereal, pretzels, and peanuts.

3. In a microwave-safe bowl or the container the candy coating comes in, melt the candy coating according to the package directions, usually 90 seconds to 2 minutes, stirring every 30 seconds, until melted and smooth. Make sure not to over-melt the candy coating because it will burn and become too thick to stir and coat the mix evenly.

4. Pour the melted candy coating over the ingredients in the large bowl and toss with a large spoon until everything is evenly coated. Pour in half the container of rainbow sprinkles and the full container of pastel confetti decors. Gently stir the mixture to incorporate.

5. Spread the mixture in an even layer on the prepared baking sheet. Immediately sprinkle with the remaining sprinkles and then the Froot Loops cereal. Allow the mixture to cool completely. Break apart and toss with the birthday hat Bugles.

BIRTHDAY HAT BUGLES

(MAKES 18)

1 container (3 ounces, or 84 g) rainbow sprinkles

8 ounces (227 g) vanilla candy coating (such as CandiQuik brand)

18 Bugles

1. Line a baking sheet with parchment paper. Pour the sprinkles into a shallow bowl. Set both aside.

2. In a microwave-safe bowl or the container the candy coating comes in, melt the candy coating according to the package directions, usually 90 seconds to 2 minutes, stirring every 30 seconds, until melted and smooth. Make sure not to over-melt the candy coating because it will burn and become too thick to stir and coat the mix evenly.

3. Once the candy coating is melted, take one Bugle at a time, holding it by the pointy tip, and dip it into the candy coating. Don't worry about coating the pointy tip. Immediately dip the coated bottom of the Bugle into the sprinkles to create a ring of sprinkles. Lay the coated Bugle on the parchment paper to dry, about 5 minutes. Repeat with the remaining Bugles.

4. Once the coated Bugles are set, hold the sprinkled end of each Bugle and dip the pointy end into the melted candy coating, then immediately dip it into the sprinkles. Set the Bugle back on the parchment paper to dry and repeat with the remaining Bugles. Let them set for about 5 minutes before serving.

BACON AND PIMENTO CHEESE–STUFFED JALAPEÑO PEPPERS

(MAKES 12)

Nonstick cooking spray

6 large jalapeños, cut in half and seeded

½ cup (120 g) store-bought pimento cheese

¼ cup (30 g) shredded cheddar cheese

2 tablespoons (20 g) bacon bits

1. Preheat the oven to 400°F (200°C, or gas mark 6). Set a baking rack on top of a rimmed cookie sheet and spray with the nonstick cooking spray. Set aside.

2. Fill each jalapeño half with 2 teaspoons of the pimento cheese and place on the prepared baking rack. Sprinkle each jalapeño half with 1 teaspoon of the shredded cheddar cheese and ½ teaspoon of the bacon bits.

3. Bake for 15 to 20 minutes, until bubbly and starting to brown.

PIGS IN A BLANKET

(MAKES 24)

Nonstick cooking spray

1 tube (8 ounces, or 227 g) refrigerated crescent rolls

24 fully cooked cocktail wieners

1. Preheat the oven to 375°F (190°C, or gas mark 5). Spray a large baking sheet with the nonstick cooking spray and set aside.

2. On a cutting board, unroll the crescent dough and separate into 8 triangles. Cut each triangle into 3 smaller triangles. Place one wiener on the wider end of each triangle, then roll it up to the opposite, pointy end. Place each pig in the blanket, pointy side down, on the prepared baking sheet.

3. Bake for 12 to 14 minutes, or until a deep golden brown. Immediately remove from the baking sheet.

PUMPKIN CHEESE BALL

(MAKES 1)

16 ounces (454 g) cream cheese (plain or pumpkin spice flavored)

2 cups (240 g) shredded orange cheddar cheese

½ teaspoon pumpkin pie spice

½ teaspoon cayenne pepper

½ teaspoon paprika

1 bell pepper stem

1. Using a stand mixer or a bowl and sturdy spoon, mix the cream cheese, cheddar cheese, pumpkin pie spice, cayenne, and paprika together until well combined.

2. Line a 1.25-quart (1.1 L) mixing bowl with plastic wrap and press the cheese mixture firmly into the bowl. Cover completely with the plastic wrap and place in the refrigerator for at least 1 hour.

3. Once the cheese ball is chilled, lift it from the bowl with the plastic wrap and place flat side down on a work surface. Leave the plastic wrap around the cheese ball, and with the tip of a butter knife, carve lines down the sides to resemble a pumpkin.

4. Lift the cheese ball from the work surface with the palm of your hand and gently remove the plastic wrap. Transfer the cheese ball to the center of the wooden board. Use the butter knife to indent the carved lines even more to look like a pumpkin.

5. Stick the bell pepper stem in the top of the pumpkin-shaped cheese ball.

NUTTER BUTTER ACORNS

(MAKES 10)

5 Nutter Butter sandwich cookies

1 cup (160 g) chocolate candy melts

½ cup (100 g) chocolate sprinkles

5 thin pretzel sticks, broken in half

1. Horizontally cut each cookie in half.

2. Melt the chocolate candy melts according to the package directions. Put the chocolate sprinkles in a shallow bowl.

3. Dip the cut side of the cookie half about a quarter of the way into the melted chocolate coating and let the excess chocolate drip off. Dip the coated end into the bowl with the sprinkles, then immediately stick the broken end of half a pretzel stick into the dipped side of the cookie so it stays as the candy coating sets. Lay on a piece of parchment paper to set. Repeat with the remaining 9 cookie halves.

LATKES

(MAKES 24)

Canola oil, for frying

1 bag (20 ounces, or 560 g) refrigerated hash brown potatoes (if using frozen hash brown potatoes, thaw and drain well before using)

3 large eggs, well beaten

1 teaspoon kosher salt

½ teaspoon onion powder

1. Heat a large skillet over medium-high heat and pour in the canola oil to a depth of ¼ inch (6 mm).

2. In a medium mixing bowl, mix together the potatoes, eggs, salt, and onion powder until well combined.

2. Scoop 3-tablespoon (45 g) portions of the potato mixture into the hot skillet and immediately press flat with the back of a flat spatula. Let cook for about 3 minutes per side, until golden and crisp on both sides. Drain on paper towels. Repeat with the remaining potato mixture, adding more oil if necessary.

MARGHERITA PIZZA DIP

(MAKES 2 CUPS, OR 250 G)

14 cherry tomatoes, cut in half

1½ cups (180 g) shredded mozzarella cheese, divided

½ teaspoon kosher salt

¼ cup (10 g) chopped fresh basil

1. Preheat the oven to 400°F (200°C, or gas mark 6). Spray an 8-ounce (227 g) casserole dish with nonstick cooking spray. Set aside.

2. In a small bowl, toss the cherry tomato halves with 1 cup (120 g) of the shredded mozzarella cheese, salt, and basil.

3. In the prepared casserole dish, layer ¼ cup (30 g) of the shredded mozzarella cheese in the bottom, followed by the tomato and cheese mixture. Top with the remaining ¼ cup (30 g) shredded mozzarella cheese.

4. Bake for 15 minutes, or until the cheese is bubbling and starting to brown on top. Keep warm until ready to assemble the board.

MINI BAGUETTE PIZZA TOASTS

(MAKES 8)

Nonstick cooking spray

8 baguette slices, cut ½ inch (13 mm) thick

8 teaspoons (40 ml) pizza sauce

½ cup (60 g) shredded mozzarella cheese

40 mini pepperoni

1. Preheat the oven to 425°F (220°C, or gas mark 7).

2. Top each baguette slice with 1 teaspoon of the pizza sauce and then 1 tablespoon (8 g) of the shredded mozzarella and 5 mini pepperoni.

3. Bake for 5 to 8 minutes, until the cheese is melted and starting to brown. Keep warm until ready to assemble the board.

CLASSIC GRILLED CHEESE SANDWICHES

(MAKES 3)

6 slices American cheese

6 slices soft white bread

Butter, to taste

1. Place 2 slices of cheese between 2 slices of bread for each sandwich.

2. Spread the outside of each piece of bread generously with butter and grill in a skillet over medium heat until the cheese is melted and the bread is golden on both sides.

BACON CHEDDAR GRILLED CHEESE SANDWICHES

(MAKES 2)

4 thick slices cheddar cheese

4 thick slices bacon, cooked

4 slices deli-style white or sourdough bread

Butter, to taste

1. Place 2 slices each of cheese and cooked bacon between 2 slices of bread for each sandwich.

2. Spread the outside of each piece of bread generously with butter and grill in a skillet over medium heat until the cheese is melted and the bread is golden on both sides.

BRIE AND FIG JAM GRILLED CHEESE SANDWICHES

(MAKES 8)

½ cup (72 g) Brie, at room temperature for easy spreading

1 large baguette, sliced into 16 rounds (¼ inch, or 6 mm, thick)

8 teaspoons fig jam

Butter, to taste

1. Spread a layer of Brie on 8 of the baguette rounds and a layer of fig jam on the other 8 baguette rounds. Sandwich the Brie sides with the fig jam sides to create 8 sandwiches.

2. Spread the outside of each side of the baguette sandwiches with butter and grill in a skillet over medium heat until the cheese is melted and the bread is golden on both sides.

S'MORES SNACK MIX

(MAKES 1¾ CUPS, OR 100 G)

1 cup (40 g) Golden Grahams cereal

½ cup (20 g) mini marshmallows

¼ cup (40 g) chocolate chips

1. In a small bowl, combine the cereal, mini marshmallows, and chocolate chips.

S'MORES DIP

(MAKES 2 CUPS, OR 220 G)

1 cup (165 g) chocolate chips

18 regular marshmallows

1. Preheat the oven to 375°F (190°C, or gas mark 5).

2. Place the chocolate chips in a small ovenproof skillet and top with the marshmallows.

3. Bake for 8 to 10 minutes, or until the marshmallows are toasted and the chocolate is melty.

HOMEMADE HUMMUS

(MAKES 1¼ CUPS, OR 300 G)

1 can (15 ounces, or 425 g) chickpeas

2 tablespoons (30 g) plain Greek yogurt

2 tablespoons (30 ml) fresh lemon juice

1 tablespoon (15 ml) extra-virgin olive oil

1 clove garlic, peeled

1 teaspoon kosher salt

½ teaspoon cumin

1. Place all the ingredients in a blender and blend until smooth.

2. Store in the refrigerator until ready to serve.

BEET HUMMUS

(MAKES 1½ CUPS, OR 360 G)

1 can (15 ounces, or 425 g) chickpeas

2 tablespoons (30 g) plain Greek yogurt

2 tablespoons (30 ml) fresh lemon juice

1 tablespoon (15 ml) extra-virgin olive oil

1 clove garlic, peeled

1 teaspoon kosher salt

½ teaspoon cumin

½ cup (85 g) chopped ready-to-eat cooked beets

1. Place all the ingredients, except the beets, in a blender and blend until smooth.

2. Add the beets and blend again until the beets are completely incorporated into the hummus—the hummus will turn a vibrant magenta color.

3. Store in the refrigerator until ready to serve.

HOMEMADE SALSA

(MAKES 1½ CUPS, OR 338 G)

10 Roma tomatoes, seeds and pulp removed

½ cup (60 g) packed fresh cilantro

¼ medium white onion, ends trimmed and peeled

½ large fresh jalapeño

1 tablespoon (15 ml) fresh lime juice

1 clove garlic, peeled

½ teaspoon kosher salt

1. Place all the ingredients into a blender or food processor. Pulse until well combined but still a little chunky. Taste and add more salt, if desired.

2. Let the salsa rest in the refrigerator for at least 30 minutes before serving.

THE BEST BLENDER GUACAMOLE

(MAKES 2 CUPS, OR 450 G)

2 cups (120 g) fresh cilantro (about 1 bunch)

¼ medium peeled white onion

2 tablespoons (30 ml) fresh lime juice (about 1 large lime)

1 clove garlic, peeled

1 medium jalapeño, stem removed (with or without seeds, depending on heat preference)

1 teaspoon kosher salt

3 large ripe avocados, pitted and peeled

1. Place the cilantro, onion, lime juice, garlic, jalapeño, and salt in a blender or food processor and blend for 1 to 2 minutes, scraping down the sides with a spatula a few times, until a smooth paste forms.

2. Add the avocados and pulse 8 or 9 times, removing the lid and scraping down the sides with a spatula every 3 pulses. The guacamole should be smooth with several small chunks of avocado. Taste and add more salt or lime, if desired.

3. Serve immediately.

PICO DE GALLO

(MAKES 1 CUP, OR 225 G)

1 cup (180 g) diced seeded tomatoes

¼ cup (15 g) chopped fresh cilantro

¼ medium white onion, diced

2 tablespoons diced jalapeño

1 tablespoon (15 ml) fresh lime juice

1 clove garlic, minced

½ teaspoon kosher salt

1. Place all the ingredients in a medium bowl and stir well to combine.

2. Store in the refrigerator until ready to serve.

QUICK AND EASY MICROWAVE QUESO

(MAKES 1½ CUPS, OR 360 G)

1½ cups (173 g) shredded medium cheddar cheese

3 tablespoons (45 ml) half-and-half

2 tablespoons (30 g) plain cream cheese

2 tablespoons (28 g) salsa (store-bought or see recipe on page 157)

1. Place all the ingredients in a medium microwave-safe bowl and stir well to combine.

2. Microwave in 30-second intervals, stirring after each interval, until melted and smooth

3. Use a wire whisk to make the queso even smoother before serving. Serve immediately.

CHILI CON QUESO

(MAKES 2 CUPS, OR 480 G)

1½ cups (360 g) queso (store-bought or see recipe above)

½ cup (120 g) canned chili

1. If using store-bought queso, place all the ingredients in a medium microwave-safe bowl and stir well to combine.

2. Microwave in 30-second intervals, stirring after each interval, until melted and smooth.

3. Use a wire whisk to make the queso even smoother before serving. Serve immediately.

4. If using homemade queso, once the queso is melted, stir in the chili.

3-INGREDIENT SOUR CREAM SPINACH DIP

(MAKES 2 CUPS, OR 480 G)

1 package (10 ounces, or 283 g) frozen chopped spinach, completely thawed and drained of juice on paper towels

1 container (16 ounces, or 454 g) sour cream

1 package (0.7 ounce, or 19 g) Italian salad dressing mix

1. Place all the ingredients in a medium and stir well to combine.

2. Let the dip set in the refrigerator until ready to serve.

SPINACH AND KALE GREEK YOGURT DIP

(MAKES 2¼ CUPS, OR 504 G)

½ cup (15 g) chopped fresh baby spinach

½ cup (34 g) chopped fresh kale

¼ cup (37 g) diced red bell pepper

¼ cup (32 g) diced carrot

1 cup (230 g) plain Greek yogurt

¼ cup (60 g) light mayonnaise

½ teaspoon garlic salt

1. Place all the ingredients in a large bowl. Gently stir together with a spatula until well combined.

2. Store in the refrigerator until ready to serve.

BASIL SPINACH PESTO

(MAKES 1½ CUPS, OR 378 G)

1 cup (40 g) packed fresh basil

1 cup (30 g) packed fresh spinach

½ cup (68 g) pine nuts

¼ cup (20 g) shredded Parmesan cheese

2 cloves garlic, peeled

½ cup (120 ml) extra-virgin olive oil, divided

1 tablespoon (15 ml) fresh lemon juice

Salt, to taste

Freshly ground black pepper, to taste

1. Place the basil, spinach, pine nuts, Parmesan, garlic, ¼ cup (60 ml) of the olive oil, and lemon juice in a food processor, and process until well combined.

2. Slowly pour in the remaining ¼ cup (60 ml) olive oil into the food processor while processing and process until smooth. Season with the salt and pepper.

3. Store in an airtight container in the refrigerator until ready to serve.

RESOURCES

Regarding the food products listed for each board, if not specified otherwise, it is a prepared item that you can buy at a store or online. Some of the grocery stores listed below may be local to my region, but you should be able to find most food items at your local large grocery store chain.

BOARDS

Sur La Table
www.surlatable.com

Target
www.target.com

Cost Plus World Market
www.worldmarket.com

Crate and Barrel
www.crateandbarrel.com

Williams Sonoma
www.williams-sonoma.com

ACCESSORIES

Sur La Table
www.surlatable.com

Target
www.target.com

Cost Plus World Market
www.worldmarket.com

Crate and Barrel
www.crateandbarrel.com

Swoozie's
www.swoozies.com

Anthropologie
www.anthropologie.com

Nordstrom
shop.nordstrom.com

FOOD

Central Market
centralmarket.com

Trader Joe's
www.traderjoes.com

Target
www.target.com

Kroger
www.kroger.com

Whole Foods Market
www.wholefoodsmarket.com

Tom Thumb
www.tomthumb.com

Walmart
www.walmart.com

Amazon
www.amazon.com

INDEX

Page references in *italics* indicate images.

ACKNOWLEDGMENTS

First of all, I want to thank YOU! Thank you so much for choosing my book as a resource that hopefully inspires you to build beautiful boards and create memorable moments around them with your loved ones for years to come. I'm excited to see the boards you create from this book and to hear all about how much fun you had building and enjoying them. I'm here for you, so please feel free to reach out for encouragement and praise. I want you to make these boards your own and be proud of yourself for creating them.

Thank you to my love, Brandon, for being my biggest supporter. I'm a more confident woman, wife, mom, and business owner because of you. Your unconditional love and encouragement mean more to me than you will ever know. Thank you for challenging me and cheering me on every step of the way. I can always count on you, and I'm so unbelievably grateful for that. Growing old with you is my dream and we're living it every day. I love you so much!

Thank you to my little loves, Baker, Bryce, Barrett, and Brookie, for filling our home with so much love, laughter, and chaos. I'm beyond blessed to be your mom. Thank you for your trust, your big hugs, your sweet kisses, your comforting cuddles, your encouraging words, and your forgiveness. Your excitement for the boards we enjoy together as a family is what fuels this passion most. And having you eagerly by my side as we build them together makes me the happiest of all.

Thank you to my mom, Susan, for showing me how to entertain and create memorable moments with others by inviting them into our home and around our dining table. And a huge thank-you for helping me so much with this book and with our kids. The long days and late nights spent shopping, sorting, counting, cleaning and, of course, snacking (your fave!) were all the more fun and memorable with you helping me. I could not have done this without you, Mom. I have felt your unconditional love and support since day one. I wouldn't be the woman or mom I am today without your example. I learn from the best!

Thank you to my dad, Bill, for instilling in me a work ethic that has served me so well over the years, for encouraging me to do what I love, and for reminding me that giving up is not an option. Thank you for being the best Pop to our kids by loving and caring for them so well. And, of course, a big thank-you for all the beautiful boards you have handcrafted for me over the years. Your boards will forever be my favorites!

Thank you to my book photographers, Jerrelle and Eric, for capturing my boards so beautifully. You are true talents and it was such an honor to work with you. Thank you for letting me take over your gorgeous studio with all my tubs, boards, and eager helpers. Your patience and attention to detail with each board meant so much to me. And your overall support and encouragement throughout this journey gave me the confidence to keep going when I needed it the most. I'm thrilled to call you friends and am looking forward to many a more late-night salty cookie and apple cobbler baking sessions.

Thank you to our dear friends, Paulette and Brittani, for your amazing friendship first and foremost. You inspire me to be a better friend. Thank you for going above and beyond to help me throughout this entire process. I didn't know how much I needed y'all until you were there for me without even being asked. I could not have done this without you. And looking back, I would not have wanted to do this without you. The memories we've created through this experience, and in our everyday adventures as friends and moms, are ones that I will cherish forever.

Thank you to my assistant, Monica, for being such a special part of our family and *The BakerMama* team. Thank you for loving us so well and for keeping me on track with all the fun and yummy ideas I have building in my brain. Having you by my side each day has helped me be a better mom and business owner. The best is yet to come!

Thank you to Kay and Kevin, for being such great friends and our favorites to wine and dine with. Thank you for your encouragement and honesty, along with your eagerness to come over at a moment's notice to enjoy one of my crazy board creations. Thank you for your support and participation in bringing this book to life. Looking forward to many more fun and delicious memories together!

And last, but certainly not least, thank you to The Quarto Group for bringing this book to life. To my publisher, Rage, for discovering me and reaching out to see if I'd be interested in doing a book. What a dream come true! Thank you for seeing my passion and for trusting me to create the amazing content that makes this book one of a kind. Thank you to my editor, Erin, for your patience as I poured my all into each board and word in this book. You brought it all together so beautifully.

Thank you! Thank you! Thank you!

ABOUT THE AUTHOR

Maegan Brown started her food blog, *The BakerMama*, in 2012, and it now has over five hundred original recipes that she makes regularly for her family and friends. She started blogging as a way of sharing her love for baking and has since expanded to share easy, family-friendly recipes, creative meal ideas, food finds, life as a family of six, and all her food board creations!

Maegan is a mother of four children, Baker, Bryce, Barrett, and Brookie, and is married to her best friend and fellow foodie, Brandon. The kitchen is the heart of their home and they love welcoming others into it. She lives in Dallas, Texas.